Tim's book is a compelling read for anyone interested in learning about resilience at the coalface, based on real-life stories and tried and tested lessons about how to manage pressure, stress and adversity. Tim takes the reader through an incredible range of experiences in some ferociously challenging situations, drawing out lessons which uncover important human traits and behaviours that can be applied to almost any personal or professional situation.

Cath Bishop – author of *The Long Win*

I loved this book. Some really practical tools to enable you to face those challenges head on.

Mandy Hickson – author of
An Officer Not a Gentleman

Practical tips to help anybody learn, improve and develop. This book will make a positive impact on your mindset, and help you bring a solutions-focused mindset to any challenge you face. It is unlikely you will face enemy fire, experience an earthquake whilst on the side of Mount Everest or attempt to tackle a stage of the Tour de France. But the lessons Tim shares from his diverse experiences can help you when facing your own enemy, mountain or gruelling endurance event. Tim can because he decided he can. Can you?

Colin Gregor – Scottish
Rugby 7's Captain

BECAUSE I CAN

I CAN

THE ROBUST GUIDE
TO BEING EFFECTIVE

TIM BRADSHAW

First published in Great Britain by Practical Inspiration Publishing, 2022

© Tim Bradshaw, 2022

The moral rights of the author have been asserted

ISBN   9781788603027 (print)
          9781788603041 (epub)
          9781788603034 (mobi)

Every effort has been made to trace copyright holders and to obtain their permission for the use of copyright material. The publisher apologizes for any errors or omissions and would be grateful if notified of any corrections that should be incorporated in future reprints or editions of this book.

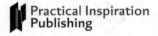

Practical Inspiration
Publishing

MIX
Paper from
responsible sources
FSC® C013604

To Dad, whose mantra was 'KBO'. I will, Dad.

"Focus on the outcome"

Filsell Wealth
2023

CONTENTS

INTRODUCTION: MAKING IT WORK

Have you ever been presented with a challenge that on the one hand is exciting and yet on the other fills you with dread and self-doubt? Have you ever been offered an opportunity either at work or at home that will require you to step firmly outside of your comfort zone? This book gives you a toolkit that will help you accept those challenges and rise to those opportunities. It won't make the challenge any easier or less daunting, but it will enable you to create resilience and overcome the hurdles that stand in your way.

If you're like me, when you're faced with a challenge, your initial reaction is to catalogue all the entirely practical reasons why you are not the right person for the job. You make very reasoned and sensible arguments as to why this challenge is better suited to somebody with more time, more experience, someone younger, or older. In other words, you focus on why you *can't* do something, rather than why you *can*.

This is true for us as individuals, but it's also true for organizations. How often have you sat in a meeting where the focus is on why something won't work? Or when something's gone wrong, the meeting might be all about finding who's to blame. The "copy all" email chain is often a way of hiding behind colleagues to avoid taking ownership of a situation, with all the risk that entails.

If you want to see challenges differently, so that you can achieve more and fulfil your full potential, you probably already know that you're going to need to change your mindset. But how?

Throughout this book we will focus on tools and techniques that give you the opportunity to make the best decisions you can and deal with situations and challenges as they present themselves. You are going to build a toolkit that can be adapted to any situation, and every challenge.

Throughout my life and career, I have wrestled with two conflicting demons. The first is a sense of overwhelming despair, the "black dog" of depression, which means I don't want to get out of bed in the morning and can see no way forward. The second is an internal drive to prove myself, to show that I can achieve whatever I set my mind to. They may seem contradictory and often they are! The result is that I volunteer for some ridiculous challenge, only to struggle to see how I could possibly see it through. It might sound unhelpful, but this inner conflict has forced me to focus on developing skills and tools to help me not only get through but, wherever possible, to thrive.

The skills and tools that I describe in this book are a collection of those that have worked for me in some of the highest pressure and most serious situations that anyone can expect to face. I don't claim to have designed them all, but I have tested them on the battlefields of Afghanistan, in an earthquake on the side of Mount Everest and whilst navigating a startup company through a global pandemic!

Nobody is born resilient. You acquire resilience with experience, determination and through failing. You can't shortcut the process or go on the resilience course. And it's not something that's a one-time deal – you have to find resilience for each new challenge. Every time you step out of your comfort zone, wanting to quit makes you human. Not giving up is what makes you extraordinary.

Whether your personal challenge is to climb Mount Everest, run your first 5 km or take that promotion at work, this book will equip you with the tools you need to succeed. They can be applied anywhere and at any time, and I'm living proof!

#BecauseICan

The so what?

This is a very simple question that we don't ask ourselves enough. Whenever we make a statement either written or verbal, we should always consider the so what. Perhaps some of the best examples of this are LinkedIn profiles or opening lines in CVs. So many of them state facts, for example: as a student I was a member of the university rugby team. Why is this relevant and what does it mean for the person reading the profile? We often write profiles or pitches for ourselves stating the facts that we think are impressive or that we have worked hard to achieve. What we should be doing is asking ourselves who is the audience and how is this relevant to them?

You often see pitches for new business or sponsorship that start with the history of the company or individual concerned. Is this relevant and what does the audience gain from it? As an example, I will use some extracts from my own LinkedIn profile. I'm certainly not saying it is perfect, but it will give you an idea.

I have always had a passion for the mountains and skiing. I have spent many hours amateur ski racing and teaching people to ski. I'd like to add this into my profile as it represents a part of my character and personality. But now as a director of an international leadership and keynote speaking company, how is this relevant? In other words, what is the so what?

Under the experience or interests section of my profile (if you don't know what I'm talking about you had better get yourself across to LinkedIn!) I could simply write: *ski instructor or loves to ski in the mountains.* This might start a conversation if the audience happened to like skiing or mountains but that would be luck. What is on my LinkedIn profile reads like this:

Tim is a BASI (British Association of Snowsport Instructors) and military qualified ski instructor. The alpine environment always inspires and challenges in equal measure. Teaching and coaching people to overcome their fears, build confidence and learn new skills in a challenging environment requires a unique and highly flexible instructional style. One that is easily adapted to the commercial coaching environment.

Tim has instructed and coached young soldiers to take their first steps into the alpine environment in the form of adventurous training. He also developed an alpine ski racing squad that won overall honours in the army ski championships even hosting Prince Michael of Kent!

Let's break that down. First, it states that I am a qualified instructor. This demonstrates a level of commitment and learning that has been recognized by a governing body. It then sets the scene explaining that as an instructor you have been operating in a non-conventional environment and are adaptable. The section goes on to explain that it means that I have developed skills that help me to be adaptable to different learning styles and help others overcome challenges and fears. The final sentence gives the audience a few interesting points to start a discussion that doesn't require them to know anything about skiing.

The so what of being a ski instructor is that I am a proficient and adaptable instructor used to working with people outside of their comfort zones. This is now directly relevant to working in any training environment. The audience no longer has to make the connections for themselves and that makes it easier to relate to or want to work with me.

A great way to help you understand the so what is to ask yourself what problem you solve. The next time you are writing a pitch, sponsorship document or profile, ask yourself what problem you solve for the person you are talking to. Of course, if you don't know what problems they might have then you will need to revert to gathering more intelligence!

For the rest of this book at the end of each section you will see the "so what". This is a guide to what action points you should take from each section.

- Avoid statements with no direction or purpose
- Ask yourself what problem you solve
- Explain who you are, not what you are.

The first two parts of the book will deal with your own ability to evaluate a challenge or respond to a high-pressure situation. They will also help you reframe an opportunity that you may feel will take you out of your comfort zone. Once these tools have been added to your kit, the following parts of the book will deal with empowering teammates and colleagues. Regardless of the situation I have found myself in, from Afghanistan to the boardroom via Mount Everest, the key factor to success has always been a because-I-can attitude combined with a great team of people.

Throughout the book you will find #BecauseICan boxes. Whilst not part of the specific content of the book they provide details on some of the challenges and organizations mentioned in the text. Perhaps they might form the basis of your next challenge?

When facing any challenge, you will need to develop skills in four key areas:

- Presentation
- Collaboration
- Negotiation
- Confrontation

Before looking at any of these areas it is critical to ensure you are only dealing with intelligence not information.

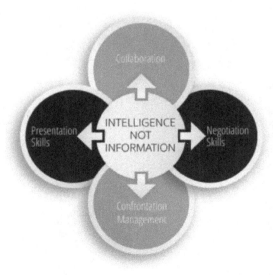

Part 1

FOCUS ON USING INTELLIGENCE, NOT INFORMATION

In the first part of the book, we are going to look at the core principle of only dealing with intelligence. We will look at filtering background information and ensuring that we are making decisions and responding to situations as they are happening.

Increasingly, we find ourselves in an ever-changing environment. We have witnessed an astonishing level of social and economic change. It covers everything from the way we communicate, to the way we interact and the way we do business. There are career paths now available to students that did not even exist as little as five years ago. It is possible to connect from almost any location on the planet and communicate whenever and wherever we choose. I will never forget walking into a tiny town in rural Tibet; we were on our way to Everest at the time and being greeted by the locals. The first thing they offered us with great pride was a can of Coca-Cola. Reaching for my phone in order to take a picture of this I then realized that I had a full 4G signal! The village had no running water and no formal sanitation. Therefore, by definition, the way that we operate needs to be adaptable to changing circumstances and situations.

As a rule, human beings don't like change. Our routines and patterns provide a degree of comfort and a handrail for us to cling to when we are unsure of a situation. When removed, it creates anxiety and can affect our behaviours. Some years ago, I served as a covert human intelligence officer. The roles and requirements are not for the content of this book. It would be inappropriate to discuss the exact exercises and procedures used to select personnel for special duties training. But the concepts behind it are interesting.

For a period of time, we were subjected to a battery of challenges and tests. Some physical, some mental and some practical. I remember running through the woods as a group and at various stages being stopped and told to perform additional physical challenges, things like carrying one of your teammates up a hill, and then you would resume running. During one such interval we were stopped and told to drink water. We were then ushered into a clearing where a car was parked with its boot open. In the boot were a series of objects that we were told to memorize. The running and exercises then resumed. You might think that this all sounds as you would expect; however we were never given any of the usual parameters. We were taken out for a run but given no idea how far or how fast we would be running. We would be told to memorize the random objects but with no idea why, for how long or what we would be expected to do with the information. We would climb into bed not knowing whether we would be there for one hour or ten. It was never ten! Our usual patterns and routines had been removed. This causes immense stress and self-induced pressure. It is a test of resilience and an ability to operate in ever-changing environments without a handrail.

We design processes that provide a step-by-step guide to almost any situation that we happen to find ourselves in. The problem is that a process is primarily designed to work in an environment that is not changing and remains stable. You only need to visit any form of major manufacturing plant to see this in action. If we are assembling a car, for example, the input of the operator is not required. The various components need to be fitted in the right sequence and at the right time with as little variation as possible. Nobody wants the one car where the operator decided to fit the wing mirror somewhere random!

The same cannot be said when we are dealing with people or fluid situations. A process simply won't be adaptable and can force us into thinking in a linear pattern. Anyone that drinks their coffee black will have experienced this. Early in the morning you walk into your favourite chain coffee store. You stand patiently in line before telling the "barista" that you would like a regular black coffee. I am then asked for my name. Frankly a dangerous thing to do if it is before 0800hrs! Almost then without a pause I am asked if I would like milk in that? My reply, of course, is that then it wouldn't be black! The reason for this confrontation is that somebody at the coffee store has designed a process for dealing with customers. The staff are then trained to follow that process without question. After a period, this becomes autonomous with the barista barely conscious of their actions. The process designed to create a great customer experience has achieved the opposite.

One way around this problem is to develop a tool kit rather than a process. Take any given challenge that you face or outcome that you wish to achieve and break it down into a series of skills. Be as specific as you can. If you need to deliver a career-changing pitch to a prospective client, break it down. Some of the skills needed might be presentation design, public speaking and negotiation. Take each skill in turn and seek to learn from an expert in that skill, not necessarily from the sector in which you work. As an example, who better to teach negotiation than a former hostage negotiator? As you acquire new skills, you add them to the toolbox of the ones that you already have. Now whenever you are faced with a different set of circumstances, rather than trying to make a process fit, you identify the outcome that you are trying to achieve and select the appropriate tools for the job.

If you follow a set process that is designed to work in a specific set of circumstances it is unlikely to be adaptable and will only be effective in a controlled environment. As discussed earlier, this is not the world in which we live and operate. The military have a fantastic expression which is that no plan survives first contact with the enemy!

So what?

- Build a tool kit not a process
- Break any challenge down into its specific component parts
- Work out the individual skills you need to accomplish a given task
- Collaborate with those who provide the missing skills or knowledge.

What is real?

Before we get into the next key area of discussion, have a go at this exercise. Allow yourself a specific time limit: 20 minutes works well. Read through the UN Rescue Mission scenario below and then by your allotted time come up with a solution to the problem. The stricter you are with yourself, the more effective this exercise will be.

UN RESCUE MISSION

The blizzards in Fifedom have finally passed and the winds abated. A year of horrific storms and blizzards have left the population with ruined houses, ruined infrastructure and severe refugee and medical problems. You and Paul Horwood travel to the country to join the staff of a small but efficient charity. The charity runs the Fifedom storm relief programme and aims to deliver much needed supplies and medicines to isolated regions, especially to medical centres and orphanages.

You arrive in the town of Tyninghame on Sunday 21 November and find yourself assigned to a team led by Tim Bradshaw. He tells you that there is a briefing at 1800 hours and asks you and Paul to attend. Having settled into makeshift accommodation, you join the others. Tim introduces you to his team: Cedric, an engineer, Clive, and Emily, a nurse. They are delighted you have arrived to replace two other volunteers who were injured in a traffic accident. With the introductions over, the briefing begins. The last convoy of the year will leave tomorrow at 0900 hours. Essential supplies of blankets and winter clothing will be taken in three trucks; medical supplies will be carried in two Land Rovers and one truck. The convoy will travel the 225 miles along route 930 to the medical centre and orphanage at Dunbar. It will stop for 30 minutes at the small village of Linton some 150 miles away. The Land Rovers will be driven by Emily and you. The weather forecast is poor: storms, freezing temperatures and the possibility of snow. The aim is to deliver the supplies to Dunbar by 1830 hours which is 30 minutes after last light.

The journey starts off well and you keep to the scheduled timings but by the time you reach Linton at 1500 hours your Land Rover and two trucks, one of which is carrying medical supplies, need to stop at a garage for repairs. Tim decides to leave you, Paul and Cedric to do the work and then to carry on to Dunbar in the morning. Before he leaves, Tim places you in charge and says he will telephone the garage later in the evening; he hopes you will not need your first-aid experience. Cedric tells you that the truck is using too much fuel and that if four-wheel drive has to be engaged, consumption will drop by half, from 8 mpg. The tank holds 38 gallons.

At 2020 hours, Tim telephones on a bad line. He tells you that Route 930 is hazardous and weather conditions are worsening. At Balmoral, he was told that the doctor is visiting some remote villages, but they hoped he would return by midday on Tuesday.

The forest road has a reasonable surface, but it is likely to be used by refugees. As a result, your speed would be reduced to 15 mph; in addition, bandits are thought to be using the woods for cover. To the east there is a drivable track: although it is heavily cratered, you should be able to manage 10 mph in a four-wheel drive. The bridge was damaged by floods last month, but has been repaired, albeit temporarily. The situation in Dunbar is horrendous: a fire has damaged the medical centre and orphanage and Emily says that the medical supplies must arrive by 1500 hours if not before. Tim tells you not to travel at night but to leave at first light which is at 0720 hours. The route is up to you but as there is no petrol in Dunbar you must take the return journey into account.

You think about the best route to take and set off at dawn, telling the others you will make a final decision on the route when you reach the junction 20 miles north of Linton. Nearing the junction your eyes are drawn to the side of the road. Slowing down, you see a woman and two children, aged about 3 and 5. They are weak, emaciated and bleeding. Just before the woman passes out, she begs you to save her children. You recognize the signs of hypothermia and realize you must act quickly.

You must assess the problem; decide your aims, consider the alternative courses open to you and arrive at your plan giving your reasons.

Fifedom

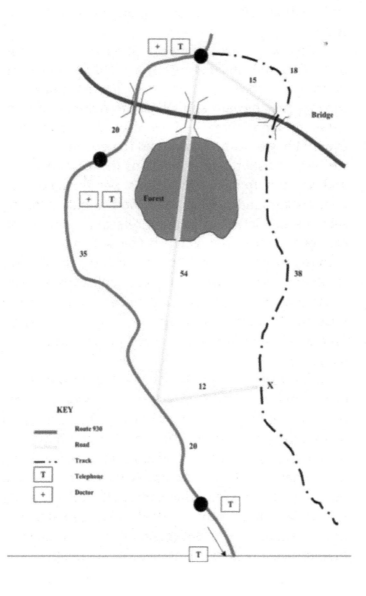

As you read through the exercise you probably experienced varying degrees of frustration, annoyance and possibly decided to give up and skip to the next section!

Why was this relatively simple problem so frustrating and difficult to work out? There is too much information. As we start to read, we are not sure which sections are relevant and which are not. The level of detail becomes more and more overwhelming and eventually we start to skim-read the document. Once we begin to skim-read it leads us to make mistakes and we jump to false conclusions. Depending on our own backgrounds, beliefs and motivations, differing sections and details will appear relevant to you. As an example, some of you will have focused on what to do with the woman and children whilst others will have spent time trying to work out fuel calculations. You can see that depending on which details you focus on, the mission emphasis and, therefore, outcomes change. This problem occurs in two directions, incoming and outgoing.

If we receive incoming, overwhelming quantities of information we will experience the same anxiety and frustration as you may have just experienced whilst trying to solve the UN Rescue Mission. You focus on the wrong elements and find yourself suffering from what we call analysis paralysis. We must take a tactical pause (more of this later) and work out what is real. We must focus on dealing with intelligence not information. In order for information to become intelligence it must be all of these three things:

- Accurate
- Timely
- Relevant.

A simple method is to go through the document with a marker pen and discard any waffle or information that does not instantly meet all three of the above criteria. You will have significantly reduced the amount of information that you need to process and increased your band width. Whenever I am planning any major challenge or task, this is always the place that we start. Ask yourself what is fact and what is hearsay or rumour.

FILTERED

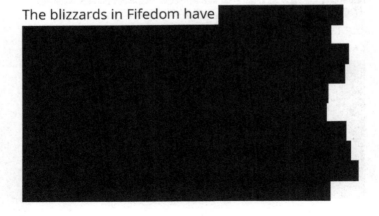

The blizzards in Fifedom have

you and Paul to attend.

Tim introduces you to his team, Cedric, an engineer, Clive Robbins, and Emily who is a nurse.

Essential supplies of blankets and winter clothing will be taken in three trucks; medical supplies will be carried in two Landover's and one truck. The convoy will travel the 225 miles along route 930 to the medical centre and orphanage at Dunbar. It will stop for 30 minutes at the small village of Linton some 150 miles away.

The aim is to deliver the supplies to Dunbar by 1830 hours which is 30 minutes after last light.

Tim decides to leave you,

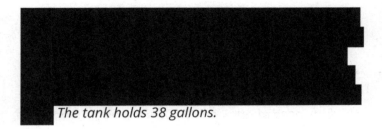

The tank holds 38 gallons.

At 2020 hours Tim telephones on a bad line. He tells you that Route 930 is hazardous and weather conditions are worsening.

The forest road has a reasonable surface but it is likely to be used by refugees. As a result, your speed would be reduced to 15 mph; in addition, bandits are thought to be using the woods for cover. To the east there is a drivable track: although it is heavily cratered, you should be able to manage 10 mph in 4-wheel drive.

Emily says that the medical supplies must arrive by 1500 hours if not before. Tim tells you not to travel at night but to leave at first light which is at 0720 hours. The route is up to you but as there is no petrol in Dunbar you must take the return journey into account.

set off at dawn, telling the others you will make a final decision

*on the route when you reach the junction 20 miles
north of Linton.*

*Nearing the junction your eyes are drawn to the side
of the road. Slowing down you see a woman and two
children, aged about 3 and 5. They are weak, emaciated
and bleeding. Just before the woman passes out, she
begs you to save her children. You recognize the signs
of hypothermia and realize you must act quickly.*

*You must assess the problem; decide your aims,
consider the alternative courses open to you and arrive
at your plan giving your reasons*

This is also a good time to start asking yourself which
elements of the problem you can influence or control
and which you cannot.

When preparing myself for the special duties
selection process, I gathered as much information
on the Unit and the process as I could find. I then
filtered it into facts or intelligence and what was
rumour or gossip. Elements such as the weights we
would be expected to carry, the minimum distances
and speeds we would have to run were relatively easy
to confirm. They were things that I could take control
of by preparing myself before selection. This provides
greater capacity to be able to deal with the unexpected
and therefore uncontrollable elements that inevitably
follow. Take any challenge or problem that you are
given and break it down into its component parts. You
can ask yourself the following questions:

- What is my outcome?
- How do I measure it?
- What are the implied tasks?
- What intelligence do I require in order to complete the task?
- What skills will I need to acquire (be thorough and specific)?
- Who should I collaborate with?
- What are my timings (start at the outcome and work backwards)?
- Any constraints?

Once you have done this what you are left with is a much more concise and less daunting view of the challenge or problem in front of you. I have found this technique to be effective for dealing with anxiety when faced with any number of high-pressure decisions or situations.

Using the UN Rescue Mission my analysis would look something like this:

First, filter out all the information that does not contribute to the solution. As an example, the first paragraph of the document, whilst setting the scene, contributes nothing to working out the solution. Next, go through the process of asking the questions listed above. Remember that each of these questions can be given to different team members to answer. Doing this makes the process more efficient and empowers the team. It will also ensure that in the discussion that follows, each team member has a clear understanding of what is to be achieved and any factors that need to be considered.

What is my outcome?
Get medical supplies to the village

How do I measure it?
Successful delivery of the supplies

What are the implied tasks?
Care of the woman and children
Plan for the return journey
Protect team and supplies

What intelligence do I require in order to complete the task?
Possible routes and distances
Intelligence assessment for each route
What fuel supplies do I have?

What skills will I need to acquire (be thorough and specific)?
Medically trained team members
Drivers
Mechanic / engineer

Who should I collaborate with?
Village receiving supplies
Local authorities
Local hospital and population centres

What are my timings (start at the outcome and work backwards)?
Depart 0720hrs must arrive by 1500hrs
Calculate timings for your chosen route

Any constraints?
Carry out a risk assessment taking into consideration things like the broken bridge, state of the roads and bandits in the woods

In March 2020 as the global Coronavirus pandemic struck, our business lost all its work for the coming year. Our mantra had been that we only deliver face-to-face business training! As a team of four directors, we sat down (via Zoom!) and asked ourselves the questions I've listed above. We focused on our why and looked for areas where we could add value. As a team, we have a great deal of experience leading people in high-pressure and often dangerous environments.

Whilst some were looking at furlough schemes and minimizing their operations, we looked for opportunity. We did our best to ignore the online rumours and focused entirely on the areas of business where we knew that we could add value. Once we had decided on our outcome and our message, we then focused on the implied tasks and intelligence gathering. What communications systems could we use? Who could help us deliver electronically? Using this approach enabled Sandstone Communications not only to survive, but to thrive. The company now has an entire digital offering called The Hub that was designed, written and produced from home during the lockdown period.

What happens if we communicate outgoing information rather than intelligence? If you have ever sent out a long-winded, rambling email it is likely that the person reading it was experiencing similar frustrations to those felt by you during the UN Rescue exercise. The last time you received an email that started with a paragraph talking about the weather, the history of the company or how much they had enjoyed talking to you during your previous call, what you were thinking all the time you were reading? You were probably thinking "what do you want?" or "get to the point"! If we are looking to influence people, this type of reaction is not a good starting point.

In addition, the reader starts to skim-read the document which causes them to pick up on certain details and miss others. The result is that we miss prioritizing things and get facts out of context.

I'm sure that whilst you were reading the initial documents you began to do this and, as a result, focused on a particular aspect of the problem, perhaps the fuel consumption or the injured woman and children. The result is that your perception of what needs to be achieved is biased to the facts that you have skim-read from the document. Only pass on what is intelligence not random information. Look at the next version of the UN Rescue document.

Aim: The aim is to deliver the supplies to Dunbar by 1830 hours which is 30 minutes after last light.

Update: Depart 0720hrs must arrive by 1500hrs

Route: Total journey 225 miles. Way point 150 miles
Route 930 – Hazardous (winter conditions worsening)
Forest Route – Good surface, busy, reduced speed 15mph (possible bandits in woods)
East route – Passable but cratered. 10mph in 4 x 4

Your team:
Cedric Engineer
Emily Nurse
Clive
Paul

Vehicles:
3 x Trucks (winter clothes, blankets and medical in one truck) 38 gallons, of fuel 18mpg if 4-wheel drive 8 mpg

2 x Land Rovers (medical supplies)

Additional considerations:
Woman and two children hypothermia

You can see that this version has been revised again. We have added value by doing some of the calculations and made the key intelligence easy to read by removing all the background waffle. The intelligence has then been presented in an easy-to-use format. This means that the document can be referred to easily when in a meeting or presenting a pitch. Whenever I am talking to potential expedition sponsors, business contacts or looking to empower my team, I always try to take a walk in their shoes. This is different to empathy. Most large companies are required to get at least three quotations when they are tendering for work. Most sports organizations are inundated with pitches for sponsorship. Sandstone receives up to ten a month! There are two critical pieces of intelligence that drop out from this. Firstly, that the person receiving the document will have to read at least three if not more very similar documents. If your document is the one that is most clear and details the intelligence most clearly, it is more likely to be read properly by the extremely busy person who must read it. The second is that most of the documents or pitches will look very similar. You should try to pass on the key intelligence that is specific to you, your idea or the project and avoid padding it out with background generic statements.

In 2018 when Paul Horwood, my Sandstone co-director and long-term adventure friend, and I were looking for a mountain guide to support our Matterhorn expedition, we found the selection process almost impossible. All their LinkedIn profiles and websites were identical. They all said "experienced, client focused, qualified mountain guide". We laughed, pointing out that what we really wanted was a grumpy, expensive guide who didn't like clients! None of them explained what they could do for us or how they differentiated themselves from any of the other guides.

So what?

When we are looking to inspire or empower teams it is even more important that we go through the process that we have discussed here. How many times have you received an email or briefing that has been "copy all" or forwarded on with little input from the sender? You read all 5,000 words and realize that two of the paragraphs were relevant to you. This also means that everybody on your team who was in the email chain has also had to spend time reading the document or listening to the briefing. A very effective way to get round this is to create a filter for the team. In other words, you read through the document. You then highlight or extract which bits are relevant to which team member. The team are then able to get directly to the sections that require their attention and action. Although you will have spent more time doing this you will have saved time and sped up the decision-making process for every other team member.

Therefore, as a team you will be working more effectively, and the team will respect you valuing their time. A theme that I will come back to in this book is that your team are like a bank account. To make a withdrawal you have to have paid in first. This is especially true when putting together teams of volunteers and helpers for large projects or expeditions.

- Only communicate intelligence
- Remove unnecessary waffle from communications
- Avoid copy all communications.

Actions on

Aged 19 I attended the Royal Military Academy Sandhurst. I certainly was not a good leader at this stage. You simply don't have enough life experience. I learned a series of lessons that were then repeated and thought out my military training. One of the most significant was the concept of designing actions on. I'm sure that most people at some stage have watched an action movie or a documentary following elite soldiers. Inevitably nothing goes quite to plan and yet the team seem to be able to pivot in a different direction and react seamlessly to changing circumstances. In the movies, this is often portrayed as quick thinking by the heroic leader, combined with unquestioning loyalty from the team. Whilst there are certainly moments in history when this has been the case, the reality is that the team have practised as many of these moments as possible. Some of them will have been practised as a desk-top exercise and some of them will have been physically rehearsed.

There is a great expression often used by military planning experts which is that no plan ever survives contact with the enemy. Leaders will spend many hours planning an operation based on what they think the enemy will do. Their manoeuvres and logistics are all put in place accordingly. The only problem is that no one told the enemy what they were supposed to do in this plan, and they tend to do their own thing! As a way of empowering the team and countering this problem, the leader and his team will spend a significant amount of time working out the "what ifs".

The leaders' plan will be based on finding the enemy at a specific location. The team will then play devil's advocate and think of as many ways as possible to mess with the plan. As each possible scenario is presented so an "action on" will be developed. In other words, the team will understand that if the enemy is not located according to plan A but is found at location B the team will carry out the appropriate action on. When this situation then occurs in the heat of battle every junior leader and team member knows exactly what to do and can adapt quickly without the need for micromanagement by the leader.

This methodology was taken to a micro level when undergoing training for specialist intelligence operations. I remember one exercise when we were setting out to meet a CHIS (or Covert Human Intelligence Source for those of you who didn't watch *Line of Duty*). Running through my head were all the possible scenarios to do with operating in a hostile environment: what happens if it's a trap, what happens if we get ambushed? The instructor turned to me and explained that the car we were driving had a puncture, and asked what was I going to do? If we stopped, I would miss the critical timings for the operation. If we stopped and were identified as soldiers, we could create an international incident. If we didn't stop, would the car fail completely? Would we draw more attention to ourselves and the operation by driving round on a flat tyre? This one simple and, with hindsight, obvious scenario had derailed my planning! As soon as our team returned to base, we got together and worked out "actions on" for as many scenarios as we could think of! Where possible, we would physically practise the actions we would take. This helped to consolidate each action and reaction.

#BecauseICan – HUMINT

Human intelligence (HUMINT) is intelligence gathered by means of interpersonal contact, as opposed to the more technical intelligence gathering disciplines such as signals intelligence and imagery intelligence. NATO defines HUMINT as "a category of intelligence derived from information collected and provided by human sources". HUMINT, as the name suggests, is mostly done by people rather than any technical means, and is commonly provided by covert agents and spies. Within the context of the military, HUMINT activity may involve clandestine activities. The subject of a HUMINT operation is referred to as a CHIS (or covert human intelligence source).

You might be thinking, how is this relevant in a business environment? Ask yourself whether you have ever been travelling to attend a pitch or negotiation and meeting your colleagues and boss in the nearest coffee shop prior to going into the meeting? Did you have a plan for what happened if one of you didn't make it or if the boss's train was delayed by an hour? Could the most junior member of the team have delivered the pitch? Similar scenarios may occur during a negotiation. Does every member of the team know what the parameters of the negotiation are? In other words, what concessions are you authorized to give? What are you authorized to give away in order to secure the deal?

The same is true on any form of expedition, especially in the hills. What do you do if one member of the group becomes ill or too tired to carry on? If the group comes across an injured climber or walker, will you sacrifice your own objectives to help? These questions are always best answered in the warm and dry where each group member can have their say and is not suffering from exposure, fatigue or summit fever.

It is unlikely that you will be able to think of every possible scenario but the more you go through this process, the bigger your catalogue of potential actions on will become.

Always debrief! I find it interesting that companies rarely debrief the wins. We are often quick to carry out a post-mortem when things have gone badly. This often has more to do with apportioning blame than improving performance. It is extremely good practice to develop a habit of debriefing. This way a debrief is seen as an opportunity to improve and learn rather than as a witch hunt. Mathews Syed's excellent book *Black Box Thinking* talks about developing a growth mindset. Seeing debriefs as a positive part of the toolkit is an extremely effective step in the direction of creating a growth mindset. You will also find that if you analyse your actions when something has gone well it is much easier to replicate.

Remember to reward the behaviours that you want to see again. I'm sure many of you will have seen the now infamous video clip of Fenton the dog in Richmond Park. If you haven't, simply type Fenton into the YouTube search box.

At some stage many of us have found ourselves trying to recall a pet dog that has decided it is having more fun charging around than sitting by its owner's feet. As we become more and more angry with the dog, it becomes less and less obedient. Eventually, the dog returns, and we chastise it for its disobedience. At first glance we have correctly disciplined the dog for its lack of obedience. Let's take a deeper look at this scenario and examine what we have done.

First, it is important to understand what it is we are trying to achieve. In other words, what is our outcome. In this case, it is to get the dog to return and to not be so disobedient in the future. This sounds rather negative. The behaviours that we want to see again are the dog returning to us. When the dog came back and we told it off, we had the opposite effect to the one we wanted. As far as the dog is concerned, it returned to the owner and got told off. Therefore, when asked to come back in the future it is even less likely to want to come back than before! If we stick to our theory of rewarding the behaviours that we want to see again when the dog returned, we should have praised it and provided an incentive to want to come back next time.

So what?

Developing an action plan for dealing with different scenarios will help any team make better decisions when they are under pressure. Getting in the habit of debriefing after every action or exercise will form good habits and create a growth mindset.

- Run desk-top exercises looking at possible eventualities
- Deal with challenging situations and conversations before they are critical
- Have a plan B and C!
- Understand your outcome
- Reward the behaviours you want to see again
- Debrief the wins as well as the losses.

Part 2

CONTINUALLY EVALUATE THE SITUATION

In order to

In this part of the book, we are going to look at removing pressure on the decision maker and ensure that we are using a looping decision-making process. We will examine why relying on a process often means that we are unable to respond effectively to dynamic events.

Be wary of process

A process can be a good thing but it's important to understand why a process exists and what it's been set up for. We often find that our teams or people we work with like a process. This is because it gives people a handrail, a system to work through.

But there's a couple of fundamental problems with relying on a process if we're trying to be effective. That is that the process itself can become part of the problem, rather than part of the solution. What happens is we become focused on the actual process, rather than the thing that we're trying to achieve, or the outcome. We create the five-step process to business development.

We turn around to a team member, and ask, "How did you get on? Did you win that new client?" The answer is often no, but I did follow all five steps.

This can often be seen in more extreme circumstances on high mountains or during specialist military selection processes. During long marches, candidates and mountaineers simply follow the person in front losing sight of what they were trying to achieve. They stop questioning whether what they are doing is the right thing, whether it is effective or whether there might be a better way of doing things. Nobody's thinking independently. There's no latitude to move left and right, and no empowerment of the team to achieve something different.

If we're creating a manufacturing process, then that's the outcome that we're looking for. If we're trying to deal with people, then there are too many variables for it to work. No two people are the same, and a set process just isn't going to work. Earlier in this book I mentioned my pet hate of being asked whether I want milk in my black coffee. That is a simple example of somebody following a set process.

If we're trying to be more effective, and we're trying to make our team more effective, we can get drawn towards a process which can be more of a hindrance than a help. The team ends up focusing on completing the process rather than achieving the outcome.

How do we get around this? What we do is create a toolkit. Look at the problem that you're trying to solve and ask yourself what skills are needed to achieve the outcome.

As an example. You need to find sponsorship for the mountain that you want to climb, or you are taking up motor racing and you need to find a sponsor to support your efforts to become the next Lewis Hamilton. You start by asking yourself, what am I going to need to do to be able to achieve the aim? This is a similar process to the one you developed during the UN Rescue Mission exercise. You decide that you will have to produce a pitch document that you can present to potential sponsors.

Therefore, in your toolkit you are going to need PowerPoint skills and to be able to speak in public. Rather than focusing on a process for finding sponsorship, you enhance the skills needed to deliver an amazing pitch.

We break the outcome down into a whole series of skills that we need to achieve, and then we put those skills into a toolbox. Then in the future when we're faced with a different challenge or set of circumstances, we look at the toolkit and ask ourselves, what skills do I need to use now to achieve the outcome, and we select the right tool for that moment in time.

After the pitch has been delivered, we debrief our performance no matter whether it was successful or not. We should focus on whether we achieved the aim and where we can improve our personal performance not on whether we correctly followed the process.

How many times have you asked a member of your team "Did you get in touch with Mrs Smith?" The response that follows is that they sent her an email. So, the answer to that question is actually, no! They followed the process but did not focus on the outcome.

As an icebreaker game to play at your next team meeting try this:

Place a pen on the table in front of a teammate.
Ask them to "try and pick up the pen".
Initially they will stare at the pen. If this happens repeat the request. They will now pick up the pen.

You explain that now they have picked up the pen, but you asked them to "try" and pick up the pen.

Place the pen back on the table and ask them to repeat the task. They will now leave the pen on the table and look at you confused!

You now explain that in fact you either did pick up or you didn't pick up the pen. The concept of trying to do something is not effective!

Using our example from above either you did speak to Mrs Smith or you didn't.

We've become focused on the act of sending the email or the message, rather than the outcome which was to talk to Mrs Smith. We think that by sending the email, we've achieved the outcome. We haven't, we've merely followed the process.

In order to become more effective, we must stop following the process and focus on achieving the outcome. Developing a toolkit of skills and contacts will help us to achieve this. In our simple example, the outcome has not been achieved until I've communicated with Mrs Smith. It sounds simple, and in essence, it is. You'd be amazed how often this is not the case. This simple change of mindset can make an enormous difference.

In Part 5 of the book, we're going to look at the differences between management and leadership, and we're going to understand that whilst both are equally important, they are distinctly different, and we should try and practice the two separately. In that chapter you will see that there is a place for developing a process, but they sit firmly in the management category. What we're going to use processes for is for measuring and monitoring, not for inspiring people.

OODA loop

If we're going to use a toolkit, rather than a process, it's important that we have a way of making that effective. One of the biggest problems we see in challenging environments now is that we've adopted a linear decision-making process. We know there's a decision we need to take in order to achieve a certain outcome. We then move in a linear fashion, directly towards that outcome.

In doing so, what happens is the pressure builds up enormously, not only on the result, not only on the decision, but also on the decision maker.

An indicator that this might be happening is when you see large amounts of "copy all" emails or "reply to all" emails going backwards and forwards. This can often be an indicator that the team members are nervous of being involved in the wrong decision especially if it goes wrong. These emails are members of the team effectively saying, "I did my bit. I did my best. If this is the wrong decision, it's not my fault".

Sometimes the pressure on the decision maker can become so great that either no decision at all gets taken and we get what we call analysis paralysis. This is because we focus so hard on the outcome of a single decision and the perceived end result that we over analyse. We stop ourselves physically taking a decision for fear of getting it wrong. Therefore, it's important that we, first, relieve the pressure on the decision maker, and then empower our team. This will give ourselves the opportunity to make the best decisions that we can.

The tool we're going to use for this is called OODA loop. First, a little bit of history. Some of you, of a certain age, will remember the film *Top Gun*. In the film, Tom Cruise plays a fighter pilot who is sent away to fighter pilot school where he will be taught to become less reliant on modern (then) weapons systems and more reliant on his powers of perception and physical skills. The film explains that the United States Navy believed that their pilots, despite expensive training, had become too reliant on process and systems rather than effective decision-making. This resulted in them losing aerial engagements! Fighter Town exists as does the school of air combat manoeuvring. It came about because of an American Air Force Colonel, John Boyd. Whilst working as a flight instructor, he was nicknamed "40 second Boyd". He challenged all comers to a "dog fight" claiming that he could defeat any opponent in under 40 seconds. He was never beaten! He believed that the pilots were blindly following a process, rather than reacting to what was happening in front of them.

To put this into context: an enemy aircraft moves into position. The American fighter pilot was trained to move to an initial attack position. They were then told that the enemy aircraft would roll in a certain direction, and that the correct response was then move into position two; this would then put them in an advantageous position, and they could take the shot. Of course, the fundamental problem with this was that nobody told the enemy fighter pilot.

If the enemy fighter pilot did something different often the American pilot would still follow the trained and rehearsed pattern. What the American Air Force was observing was that their overly process-led pilots were following their training on instinct and blindly. This meant that now they were totally out of position because the enemy aircraft hadn't responded as they've been taught that it would do.

In order to solve this problem, Colonel Boyd designed a decision-making system called OODA loop. This system enabled him to react to exactly what was happening in front of him, rather than following a set step-by-step system.

OODA stands for
Observe
Orientate
Decide
Act.

The key to understanding this is to realize that it's a loop, not a linear process. In other words, no one decision or action is the be all and end all. In fact, each decision is merely one of many decisions that form part of a constantly evolving response to what is actually happening in front of you rather than what you thought was happening or what might be happening.

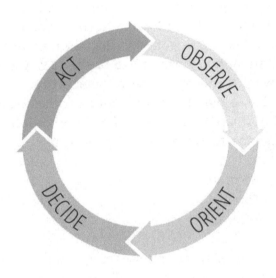

OODA loop can be applied in any situation. If you find yourself in a situation requiring immediate action, such as those encountered by fighter pilots, you apply each step in rapid succession, almost using it as a checklist. In order for this to be really effective you must pause as little as possible before re-entering the loop. If you have more time available, it can be used as a more prolonged analysis tool whereby you can involve members of your team at each step.

The first step of the OODA loop is the observation phase, or if you like, the intelligence gathering phase. We can start to empower our teams at every phase of this system.

During this phase of the loop, we are going to gather as much intelligence as possible and observe what is going on around us. The key is to only note what is intelligence, or what you're observing. Later in the book, we're going to discuss fear, and false expectation, but at this stage of the OODA loop, we only want to make a note of what we're observing and what is real. Focus on dealing with intelligence not information. In order for information to be intelligence it must always be three things:

- Accurate
- Timely
- Relevant.

If it's not all three of those things, then the chances are that it's background information, rather than specific intelligence.

As an intelligence officer, something we learned very early on was that very few people were interested in the sexy aspects of how you collect intelligence, who you'd met, where you'd met them or how you met them. All that mattered was the report that was produced at the end of the mission. In other words, the presentation of the actual intelligence was the outcome, not the process of acquiring it. If that intelligence wasn't accurate, timely and relevant, then it was not actionable, and therefore it has no value to it.

We can start to empower and involve our team right from this first stage of the OODA loop. My company, Sandstone Communications, only delivered face-to-face training. We didn't believe in online training or e-learning. Then Coronavirus happened! Just like huge numbers of companies, we suddenly found ourselves with communication systems that were ineffective. Traditionally, large law firms, as an example, meet their clients in their posh offices in London, and all of a sudden those firms, Sandstone included, were unable to communicate with their clients on a face-to-face basis.

The answer was going to be to use video conferencing and social media platforms such as Zoom, Teams or WhatsApp; not traditional solutions and certainly not those usually favoured by the more mature members of most organizations. We all needed to gather intelligence and do it quickly. The solution for us was to begin the OODA loop process. We told our younger and more tech-savvy team members that the outcome was to be able to deliver seminars and training virtually. We then asked them to gather intelligence on available platforms, compatibility, cost and, of course, what other people were doing. The team was therefore actively involved in being part of the solution and ultimately the outcome from the very outset.

Phase two is the orientation, or evaluation, phase. During the first phase we looked at gathering intelligence or observing what was happening to us. More of that again later. Now what we need to do is take that intelligence and evaluate what we can learn from the observations we made, or the intelligence that we gathered. This is a great opportunity to empower all your team members. Tell them what the outcome is that you're trying to achieve. Tell them why we're trying to achieve that outcome. Then ask them what is that intelligence telling us? How is it going to contribute to whatever it is that we're trying to achieve? It's important at this stage to remember that we're only going to orientate or evaluate the actual intelligence that we gathered during the observation phase. A top tip for me at this point is to only focus on what you can do, and what does take you towards achieving your goal, or your outcome.

When we do evaluation or analysis, it's easy to focus on what we can't do or what won't work. We hear comments like "This would be better if we had these available resources or that available equipment". You'll see this in the media quite a lot, and certainly during the pandemic; there's been a huge amount of focus on what hasn't been achieved, what hasn't been done, where PPE wasn't sent. The problem is that focusing on the negative doesn't get us any closer to achieving the outcome or the goal. So, in other words, what we're going to do is focus entirely on what it is we can achieve.

Let me give you an example. We were on the side of Mount Everest in 2015: that was when the largest earthquakes and subsequent avalanches ever to hit the Tibetan and Nepalese regions landed. I don't want to dwell on it here, but over 7,500 people were killed in the region and over 200 climbers were killed on the side of the mountain as a result of the catastrophic events. The story of our climb of Everest is a story for another day, but we found ourselves at base camp with everything destroyed around us: lost kit, lost equipment, lost people with potentially no way home. We'd come in via Kathmandu, Tibet and into the Tibetan side of Basecamp, retracing Mallory's footsteps. Suddenly, all those routes home were gone. All the paperwork that we had, including correct visas and passes, were now no longer valid, and weren't valid for any of the routes we might want to take home.

It would have been really easy at this stage, and certainly no one would have told us off, to sit down, cry into our beer and wonder about what had gone wrong? What could have been or what should have been? But, in fact, what we did was focus on what we did have available, what could we do, what routes home were available to us. So we asked ourselves questions like: What equipment do we have left? How many days' worth of rations and water have we got left? What routes are there available to get us back home? Even in those most extreme of circumstances every member of the team was a part of the solution. They were evaluating the available equipment, intelligence and resources working towards solving the problem. If you can do that, two key things happen. First, the team creates a sense of direction which creates momentum and the mission keeps moving forwards. Second, it gives each member of the team empowerment: every member of the team becomes part of the solution and takes ownership for their part in the solution.

The third part of the OODA loop is the decision. This is where we're going to look at the evaluation that we've made, check it with the intelligence that we've gathered and start to decide on whatever it is that we need to do next. Two or three things are critical here. First, it's good, old-fashioned Sandhurst doctrine to run at least three courses of action. Whatever decision you thought you were going to take, check at least two other alternatives. If I was choosing to go up the middle, I would look for a left option and a right option as well. What this will do is it will keep you honest with your decision-making process, even though it's entirely possible that what happens is you go back to your original decision. At least now you know that that probably was the correct decision to take. This is important as we find ourselves working in hybrid environments or working where our teams are scattered remotely across different locations. We can become very focused on what it is we need to do, what we need to achieve and a particular solution. Some people refer to it as an echo chamber. So to force ourselves to look for at least two other alternatives, and ask our team to contribute towards those two others, means that we are definitely checking all of the available information that comes towards us.

I'm now looking to gain empowerment to get my team and colleagues firmly behind the decision that I'm going to take. Before I formally take a decision, I'm going to get their commitment to the outcome and their ownership of responsibility. Imagine that we're about to take a decision, and I'm sitting with two other teammates. I say to my two teammates: "Right X, if I take this decision, your role within that decision is going to be to achieve 1, 2, and 3. Is that okay with you? Is that something that you think you can achieve?" X then explains to me that they think they will be able to achieve 1 and 3 but will need some support with 2. I then turn to Y and I say, "Y, are you able to support X with 2 if he takes responsibility for 1 and 3?" Y then accepts responsibility for helping X with 2. It is important to clarify the position with a summary. I explain that if we take this decision, X is going to achieve 1 and 3, and Y and X together are going to achieve 2, in order to create the required outcome. Are we all in agreement? Once X and Y confirm that they are all in agreement, we formally take the decision. It may sound like a simple thing, and you're effectively just changing round the order, but what you're doing is getting personal confirmation from each member of your team that they totally understand what it is they need to do, what their role is and, more importantly, that they're comfortable to carry out that part of the plan or the operation. You then take the decision, and the whole team goes off to carry out his own parts of that operation. We're going to discuss delivering an "in order to" later on in this book.

Now, the final phase of the OODA loop is the action phase. This is where we carry out the decision that's been made. It's my personal belief that this is the one area where we can sometimes make the single biggest difference. I've seen a plan fail on a number of occasions, not because it was the wrong plan or a terrible idea, but simply because it wasn't carried out with enough conviction to ensure success. You should carry out the action like your life depends upon it. In other words, go for it 100%, because otherwise what happens is we tentatively take a decision. We then tentatively start to carry out the action and the action itself is not successful because we haven't fully committed to it. If we carry out the action, like our life depends on it, we're giving our decision the best possible opportunity of achieving the outcome that we were focused on. This is where we go back into the loop. We carry out the action to the very best of our ability and then straightaway we start to observe the effects of that action. We've now moved into the second loop of our OODA loop. Only now, what we're doing is we're observing the effects and the intelligence of the results of our decision, and our subsequent action. We're then going to re-evaluate what has happened because of that action, re-evaluate the decisions that were made, and we go back round the loop again.

A good example of this is how the World Health Organization and local governments respond to a global pandemic. The government observes infection and hospitalization rates rising steeply. They've gathered the intelligence. They make an evaluation; they look at several courses of action. The course of action that they choose to take is for a national lockdown. They check the evaluation. They ask each of the services and providers involved whether they could carry out the required actions. They confirm that they are. The decision is then taken to go into a national-level lockdown. We lock the country down and we move back into the observation phase. We observe whether the lockdown is having an effect on the infection and hospitalization rates. Yes, it is. So, then we re-evaluate. Can we release the lockdown? No, because the rates haven't dropped sufficiently, but it is working. So, we're going to stick by our original decision for a bit longer. We start the loop again and continue to observe. Now, we evaluate that the data tells us that the numbers have dropped to a much safer level. The decision is taken to ease lockdown rules. You can see that the process continues to loop. Now, our decision-making process is guided by what is happening. It is informed by the intelligence we've gathered and as result of the actions that we've taken. So, in other words, we're responding directly to what's happening in front of us.

The significant outcome of using this OODA loop methodology is that no one decision is ever the final decision. As soon as we've taken a decision, we go back into the OODA loop, and we re-evaluate. If we need to adjust our decision or take a different action, we adjust accordingly. Rather than taking a single decision with a hope of ending up at a specific outcome, what we do is a rolling evaluation and decision process that continually adjusts what it is that we're trying to achieve and how we're trying to achieve it. This relieves pressure on the decision maker. It relieves pressure on the outcome, and it empowers the team members to work through the solution together.

So what?

Understand that when taking on challenges or stepping outside of your comfort zone you are going to have to continually evaluate the effects of actions and decisions, this is a good thing and provides the opportunity to empower the whole team whilst relieving pressure on you and other decision makers. Constant adjustment of the plan is more likely to take you towards the result that you are looking for than sticking rigidly to a plan or decision that was made early in the process.

- Continually evaluate the effects of each decision
- Empower your team at each phase of the OODA loop system

- Make sure you have the support of the team before carrying out a decision
- Carry out your decisions like your life depends on it.

Collaborate and empower

In recent years, collaboration has become a bit of a buzzword. Companies are looking to collaborate with their clients to form partnerships with their suppliers and make it appear as though the traditional seller-retailer relationship has become more of a collaborative one. I believe that we become much more effective when we collaborate on a much deeper level, not only with clients and suppliers, but with teammates, colleagues and leaders.

Ask yourself a really simple question. Do you have a "go-to" team? If a problem or a major challenge lands on the desk in front of you, do you have a group of friends or colleagues that you always turn to? You turn to them with good reason, because they always deliver and find a way to solve the problem. They always come back to you and get the results that you need.

In other words, they've become your go-to team. There is not necessarily anything wrong with this, provided that the problem or the challenge that you've put in front of your "go-to" team they are equipped to deal with. We're going to have a look at using collaboration as a way of empowering other team members, and using the wider team and organizations, possibly even clients to problem solve. Not only that, but problem solve in a way that empowers people and enables them to become part of the solution. This increases both the motivation and resilience of the team and the individual. We spoke earlier in the book about intelligence not information. We agreed that in order for information to become intelligence it must be accurate, timely and relevant. This is all well and good, provided you have, first, the required intelligence, and, second, the required skill sets to solve the problem that faces the team. What happens if the intelligence you have is incomplete, or the set of skills required to solve the problem that faces you lie outside of your existing team or your go-to group of people. It stands to reason that we perhaps need to find different team members or collaborate externally in order to fill the gaps.

Whenever you're faced with a problem or a challenging situation, the first thing we need to do is take a tactical pause, take just a second to gather yourself and collect your own thoughts. It's important to make sure that you're okay personally. Later in the book we discuss the airline emergency action of putting on your own oxygen mask first. After all, if you're not able to help yourself it is unlikely that you'll be able to empower or motivate your wider team members. Once you've done this, then you're going to evaluate the situation. In the next chapter, we will look at adding tools to the kit that will enable us to better take a tactical pause, and evaluate the situation when we are under pressure, or feel ourselves becoming afraid. As you evaluate the problem in front of you, you start to realize that there are gaps in the intelligence that you have available to you, and it may be that you need skill sets that don't already lie within your usual team. This is exactly what happened to me when one afternoon we decided we wanted to climb Mount Everest in order to shout from the highest place on Earth that it is okay to ask for help.

You see the problem is, when you ask brave soldiers, airmen, and sailors if they are okay, the answer is, inevitably, "Yes, sir, I'm fine". Therefore, we wanted to pick a physically demanding and tough challenge in order to deliver the message that it was okay to not be okay. Standing on the highest point on Earth, and shouting this message aloud, seemed like a logical place to be at the time. There are several problems with this plan. First, I've never really done any mountaineering at all and, second, I knew even less about high-altitude mountaineering or how you went about climbing Mount Everest. In this extreme situation, it's therefore obvious that I'm going to have to collaborate. I'm going to have to learn new skills in terms of mountaineering and survival in a high-altitude environment. I'm going to have to collaborate in terms of finding partners, sponsors, and expertise in order to help me plan and execute this ambitious expedition. As I've never done this before, or anything like it, I clearly had no go-to team.

The problem was broken down into a series of intelligence gaps and skills gaps. What information did I need to know in order to even start planning this mountaineering expedition and what skills was I going to need in order to be able to carry it out? This then forms the basis of collaboration. I went looking for people who were able to either fill the intelligence gaps or provide the skills to the team.

The same is true in a business context. If we're an ever-changing environment and we are presented with a problem, break that problem down into its component parts and ask yourself, where are the intelligence gaps, and where are the skills gaps within my own team? This is going to be the starting point for your collaboration. In other words, you're going to look within the business, and occasionally externally from the business, for people that may be able to provide the required intelligence and train or deliver the skills that you don't have internally.

It's also worth noting that the skills that you're looking for may well be within your team. It's just that they've never been used before. You are therefore not aware of them. A particularly good example of this was Sandstone Communication's requirement to be able to deliver training and communicate with its client electronically as lockdown was implemented. Having prided itself on only delivering face-to-face, interactive workshops this was clearly going to be a challenge for the leadership team. Rather than seek to solve the problem ourselves, the directors realized that the members of our team best placed to deliver a solution were the younger members. They were made more familiar with modern electronic communication systems and, of course, social media. Therefore, the directors began to collaborate with much more junior members of the team in order to solve the problem. Those junior members had not only the intelligence but also the required skills to solve the challenge that faced the company at that time.

When we collaborate in this way, the effect is twofold. First, it ensures that we don't simply do something the way we have always done it. Regularly, when I ask members of the board or delegates attending training courses why is it that they do something a particular way, the answer comes back simply because that's how we've always done it. By seeking to collaborate, outside of our team, with people that we perhaps wouldn't normally communicate or collaborate with, we stand a much greater chance of finding a more modern, innovative and effective way of solving whatever challenge it is that's facing us.

The second outcome is that we empower and motivate those people who we seek to collaborate with. Ask yourself, how do you feel when a team member or member of your family comes up to you and asks your opinion; when somebody says to you, "Oh, you're really good at that and I was just wondering, would you mind giving me some advice?" or "I've noticed that you do a lot of something. I would really appreciate the ability to pick your brain". We instantly feel valued and authenticated. It empowers the individual and provides the sense that they are contributing and that they are a critical part of the team. They feel like part of the solution. This is particularly effective when you are an older or more senior member of the business seeking to lead younger generations.

Now, not only are we solving a challenge that faces us, but we are, in fact, motivating our team members, creating a unifying purpose, and, therefore, building resilience.

So what?

We seek advice from those we trust and who have greater experience than ourselves. When undertaking any major challenge or leaving our comfort zones, finding a trusted adviser can be an effective way of reducing pressure on ourselves and learning from the experiences of others. This greatly speeds up our ability to learn new skills and face high-pressure situations. Seeking the advice of other team members gives them a greater sense of purpose and in turn increases team cohesion.

- Try and avoid having a "go-to" team
- Seek to fill intelligence and skills gaps
- Use collaboration to empower and motivate.

Part 3

RELIEVE PRESSURE TO INCREASE PERFORMANCE

In this part of the book, we will look at coping with pressure, fear and dealing with the fight or flight mechanism. We will examine how it is important to relieve pressure not add it in order to increase performance.

False expectation appearing real

When we set out to achieve a goal, whether that's business or personal, fear can be one of the most debilitating factors, and, in fact, it can be the fear of failing that stops us even starting in the first place. I once remember a Special Forces instructor telling me that the biggest failure rate on selection wasn't the rate of people that started the course and didn't get to the end of it, but rather the number of people that would perhaps like to try that never attempt it in the first place. It is my belief that it is the fear of the unknown and the fear of change that are the root causes of most people not taking on bigger challenges. Are we scared of the dark or are we scared of what we can't see? Are we scared of swimming in the ocean waters or are we scared of not knowing what it is that's beneath us?

In these situations, our imaginations run wild, and we create possibly doomsday scenarios. In other words, we're responding to a false expectation. We use an acronym, FEAR, standing for False Expectation Appearing Real. Often what is stopping us is the 'coulda, woulda, shoulda'... this might happen, that could happen. If I do this, this might happen and that might lead to something else happening. None of these things are real or happening. We're paralysing ourselves by responding to things that haven't happened yet and may not happen ever. They are a false expectation of the future. I wonder how many people have heard friends say things like "I didn't do that because I was worried about what other people might think" or "I didn't start that climb, because I was worried, I might not be able to finish it". None of these things are fact or real and yet they have caused us to not act.

It is important to remember that what triggers a stress reaction in one person may not have the same effect on somebody else and vice versa. Just because you are not scared by a particular situation doesn't mean that somebody else isn't.

I can walk along the summit ridge of the Matterhorn, with a 4,500 m drop straight down and I'm reasonably comfortable. Present me with negative feedback or an online tax return and it creates enormous anxiety in me. It's not better or worse; it's just different. Whenever you feel that a situation is closing in on you, the first thing you've got to do is get rid of false expectation. We can revisit the first step of our OODA loop at this point, the observation phase. More specifically, we can look at intelligence not information. Ask yourself, what is real and what is fact? As you feel your heart rate start to rise and you feel anxiety, say to yourself, "What are the facts and what is real in this situation? In this situation, what is it that I really need to deal with right now?" If you do that, one of two things will happen. Either you will realize that it was your perception of the situation that was causing you the biggest problem, and it's okay, this is obviously the best possible outcome. Or you will free up bandwidth and enhance your ability to problem solve.

A great way to think about this is, over the last 18 months during the pandemic we've all been trying to use broadband in a much bigger way than we have done before. You are desperately trying to log in to Teams to have a business meeting. The children are trying to stream Netflix or play online gaming with their friends. Your grandma has suddenly found WhatsApp and the internet just won't work. In order to free up enough capacity to enable you to operate

Teams, you've got to shut down some of those other services that are using the internet. Whilst in high-pressure and high anxiety situations, you've got to do the same thing. The first thing you want to get rid of is the false expectation. What is my perception? What is not real? What are my actual timelines? So, in other words, we're going to offload all the things that we don't need to be doing right now. What we're going to get left with are the things that are important, or mission critical for what we need to achieve. By getting rid of all the other things, we've increased our ability to deal with the more difficult challenges. Just like your home network, you've made broadband available to deal with a priority situation. There is nothing wrong with writing these things down. For me, the act of getting out my notebook and a pen seems to start the process of focusing and allowing me to concentrate on the things that are important. When I feel anxiety or I feel the pressure coming on, I stop myself, take a tactical pause and ask myself, what's real here? What is the intelligence, not the information? Then, I start to write those things down.

So what?

Whenever you start to feel nervous or anxious, remind yourself to focus on the intelligence not the information. Work out what is real and what is just your perception of a situation and then only deal with the immediate situation.

- When you feel FEAR focus on what is real
- Avoid focusing on what might happen.

#BecauseICan – The Matterhorn

The Matterhorn is an iconic 4,487m tall mountain in Switzerland. It is depicted on the packet of a Toblerone chocolate bar. The Matterhorn was one of the last of the main Alpine mountains to be climbed, not because of its technical difficulty, but because of the fear it inspired in early mountaineers. It was first climbed in 1865 from Zermatt by a party led by Edward Whymper. It took Edward seven attempts before finally reaching the summit. The expedition ended in tragedy when four of its seven members fell to their deaths on the descent. Several climbers die each year due to a number of factors, including the scale of the climb and its inherent dangers, inexperience, falling rocks and overcrowded routes. The Matterhorn is thus amongst the deadliest mountains in the world. By the late 1980s, it was estimated that over 500 people had died whilst attempting its summit since the 1865 ascent, with an average of about 12 deaths each year. In the 2000s, fewer people died each year on the mountain: this has been attributed partly to a greater awareness of the risks and partly to the fact that a majority of climbers now use local guides. However, in the summer of 2018, at least ten people died on the mountain.

Fight or flight

It's important to understand what happens to the body when we're put under stress. One of the things that can really mess with our ability to be more effective is analysis paralysis brought on by our reaction to stress, nervousness and to fear. Having an understanding as to when something is a choice or a learned reaction and when something is an involuntarily reaction to automatic processes taking place within the body is important and can enable us to better manage stress reactions in ourselves and our teammates.

I'm certainly not a biologist so I'm going to explain this section in layman's terms. This section of the book will, in simple terms, help you to understand the difference between what happens when we reward the behaviours that we want to see again and a chemical reaction that takes place when a fight or flight mechanism triggers.

In the first section of the book I mentioned Fenton, and we talked about what happens if the misbehaving dog comes back, and we tell it off. We have, in effect, just held the dog off for demonstrating the behaviour that we actually wanted him to repeat, that is, coming back again. So, it's important to understand that if we want to see positive behaviours, we must reward positive behaviours. In this example, Fenton (or in real life our team members) doesn't receive any chemical injection from the body for the action that took place. In fact, the positive feelings that they get come as a reward from the praise that we've given them rather than any automatic reaction that takes place in the body.

The fight or flight mechanism is the opposite. It is an automatic response to a hazardous situation that fills our bodies with hormones and causes a number of physiological changes to take place. In other words, it chemically and physically causes changes within the body that are outside of the individual's control. If we perceive a stressful or fearful situation, we trigger the body's fight or flight mechanism. We've all been there. What happens is that when adrenaline is released within the body, our heart rate picks up and therefore our blood pressure increases. Our body is physiologically preparing itself for a fight or to run away. Our hearing sharpens, our vision sharpens focus, and we move into a heightened state of readiness. I'm sure we've all felt that kind of tingling feeling and nervous energy within our bodies when this starts to happen. More glucose is released into the system, so we're putting more sugars into the body. We're making our body as prepared as it can be for whatever comes next. If that event or period of time is elongated and goes on for more than a few seconds, the body then starts to release cortisol into the system. Cortisol is a natural painkiller. I'm sure some of you have probably had that injected to various knees or elbows as you've got older. It also enables us to close down systems within the body that aren't required right here right now. This includes systems like our digestive system and randomly our nails and our hair stop growing. All of this is because the body is focusing everything on dealing with the immediate threat in front of it.

For those of you old enough to remember Star Trek or Star Wars, it's the equivalent of the captain of the starship telling the crew to transfer all power to the main shields. This is because at that moment in time the only thing that matters is repelling the attack. Any of the other systems that require power are secondary to defending the starship. This is exactly what takes place within the body. Now you might think to yourself: okay, but how is that relevant to me in a workplace situation or a team-building situation? The thing that's interesting is that the body hasn't really adapted over time. In other words, our fight or flight mechanism is designed to help us deal with life-threatening, exceedingly hazardous, often physical, situations such as being attacked by a sabre-toothed tiger or invaded by another marauding tribe coming to take our food or shelter. That system hasn't really adapted to things like not getting enough likes on Instagram or receiving a poor quarterly performance review. If we become stressed or anxious, we trigger the same system and therefore the same chemical reaction as if we were being attacked. Our blood flow increases, our heart rate increases, and we are involuntarily pushed chemically and physically into a state of high alert; we become super focused and sensitive. All of these things are excellent if it is a physical threat that we're about to face. This response is not necessarily useful, if the "threat" that we're responding to is a professional or personal one that requires intelligent problem solving. If the solution to the problem we face is complex but we've been put into fight or flight mode, we are not in the best position to be making good decisions or looking after our teammates.

Let me give you an example. You're sitting at your desk – whether that's at home or in the office – and you receive that phone call or email. The boss says, "Be in my office in 20 minutes". Of course you instantly think to yourself, "Fantastic this must be great news. I'm going to get promoted. I'm going to get a huge pat on the back, probably some sort of bonus, and maybe upgrade in my company car". Of course that's not the reaction that most of us have. In fact, what happens is our heart rate picks up. We instantly start to focus on what it is we might have done wrong in the last 24 hours. We delete our emails and clear our call history. We prepare ourselves for bad news. We, or rather the boss, have triggered the fight or flight mechanism. We're now in a heightened state of aggression and anxiety before we even go into that meeting. Something as simple as not communicating effectively in an everyday work situation can trigger the fight or flight mechanism within our colleagues, teammates, and friends. Once that system has been triggered, until it has been allowed to dissipate, which can take anything between 20 minutes and several hours, it is very unlikely that we're in the best possible position to solve problems, collaborate, and to communicate effectively, particularly in a complex environment. Therefore, if our priority is to get the team thinking and operating effectively and as quickly as possible the first thing we must do is to manage the effects of the fight or flight mechanism.

Of course, should you find yourself clinging to the side of Mount Everest, or desperately trying to cross a crevasse on the side of Mont Blanc, the fight or flight response that requires a physical and instantaneous reaction is not necessarily a bad thing. It's just that usually in a business or family context that's not the problem that we're facing. There are a number of factors that we can control in order to avoid triggering the fight or flight response in our teammates. Take a walk in their shoes: ask yourself, how would I feel if I was about to deliver that message? What situation are they currently in? Are they tired? Have they been under pressure or facing challenges in their personal lives? All of these things will affect how they're going to respond to how you communicate with them and will potentially trigger the stress response. So, ask yourself, how you can best alleviate or prevent that stress response from happening in the first place? Use our simple example: if I was to pop into their office and say, "Hey, it's me, just wanting to catch up for 30 minutes. Nothing too serious for us to worry about", we will prevent the triggering of that stress response and therefore end up with a far more productive meeting. When we find ourselves in a situation and we realize that that stress response has already been triggered in one of our teammates, then the first thing to do is to deal with the fight or flight response. We need to put them at their ease, relieve pressure, and reassure them that everything is going to be okay. Even if the news is not good, we can still provide reassurance and enable them to become part of the solution. Consider taking a tactical pause and maybe a change of physical or emotional scenery. We are trying to help them withdraw from that stress reaction. As a team, we can then start to move towards complex problem solving and collaborating with other team members, as we need.

If we're not careful, it's possible to create a cascade stress reaction that will run through our entire team, or even our entire organization. Using our simple example, you get the phone call – be in my office in 20 minutes – and your stress reaction is triggered. You go to the boss's office and you're already in combat mode, defensive and possibly aggressive before you even hear what they have to say. The boss perceives your stress reaction which in turn triggers their fight or flight response. What should have been a constructive debrief turns into a confrontation that further enhances your stress reaction. You then leave the boss's office, and you go back down to your teammates, and you tell them to be in your office in 20 minutes for a debrief. We've now triggered the same stress reaction in our teammates and the cycle now repeats itself. What should have been a constructive debrief again turns into a confrontation. Only now we've triggered the stress reaction in a team of ten people. They then go out to talk to their team members, and on it goes.

So within our team, and even our wider organization, we've now got an entire group who are at the mercy of a chemically enhanced stress reaction, all of which they can do nothing about. This does not put them, the team, or the organization in the best possible position to deal with whatever situation is happening directly in front of them, unless of course you have been attacked by a sabre-toothed tiger! It's really important that we identify when this might be happening and we put in an air gap. Creating a tactical pause and allowing the fight or flight mechanism to dissipate will move the team more quickly to a situation where it is able to function at full capacity. Using our Star Trek analogy, we can move the power from defence shields back to the life support systems. This will help prevent analysis paralysis and make us far more effective at dealing with whatever problem may be presenting itself.

Whenever I'm leading a team or working with an affiliated group of people, I try to identify when the fight or flight or stress reaction is occurring. I then find it easier to remind myself that that person is experiencing a chemical reaction to something that has caused them anxiety that is beyond their control. So, in other words, they're subject to an autonomous chemical reaction, rather than them making a choice to be aggressive or argumentative with me. I then see it as my role to defuse that situation in order to create reassurance and to help them come down out of that state of heightened alertness, so that we as a team can then collaborate and move forward.

When that stress reaction is happening with me personally, I also try to understand what that is and then do my best to deal with that response mechanism before I try and communicate or collaborate with my team members. As an example, in 2018 as Paul and walked up onto the summit ridge line of the Matterhorn, where the fall was 4500 metres straight down, and the only thing protecting us was the handheld rope between me and my guide Andy, my heart rate started to increase, my anxiety levels rose, and my vision and hearing became super sensitive to what was going on around us. The reaction that I needed to deal with that situation was one of calm and control, in order to make deliberate movements. I focused on the FEAR acronym, pushed aside the false expectation, and took several deep, slow breaths. I looked down at the track that I was walking on and fed myself intelligence, not the information, and reminded myself that all I needed to do was to keep putting one foot in front of the other and then there was nothing technical required of me. I reminded myself that it was my perception of what might go wrong that was causing me anxiety. I'd be a liar if I said that that made everything completely okay, but it started to allow me to come back down from the stress reaction and to gain a much more calm, controlled demeanour. It enabled me enough control to react better to the situation that was in front of me.

We're all familiar with the briefing when we get on an aeroplane. We are told to put on our own oxygen mask before attempting to help others. The reason for this is that if you're not in a fit state personally, your ability to assist anybody else is greatly reduced. Therefore, never be afraid when you feel that stress reaction happening in yourself to take a minute, or a tactical pause as we like to call it, to deal with that reaction within yourself first. There are two or three tips here. I'm always mindful of telling people how to react to stress. There are volumes of books written about being in the moment, wellness, Pilates, or whatever works for you. But my tip is that there is no silver bullet. Find a system or a process that works for you, whatever that looks like.

There is some merit to using physical exercise. There's a strong argument that says that the fight or flight mechanism primarily exists to enable us to deal with a physical threat or a physical response to a particular situation, to run away to have a fight. Taking a moment and doing some light physical exercise is one way of helping to reduce that stress reaction – take a walk around the block, step outside and get some fresh air, whatever that might be. Find a way that works best for you to deal with the situation. Whenever you feel that anxiety, increased blood flow, racing pulse rate, reach into your toolkit, find your coping strategy, and use it. Do this before you do anything else. Once you feel yourself start to slow down, you will find that your ability to concentrate and to think in a wider, more problem solving manner will increase. Therefore, your ability to deal with the problem in front of you will be enhanced. That is the moment at which you can start to collaborate and get support from other people.

So what?

I have found myself in a number of scary situations over the years, from gun fights in Afghanistan to earthquakes on the side of Mount Everest. No amount of exposure to these situations has reduced the effects of the fight or flight mechanism or stopped it from being triggered. The system is designed to protect us and is therefore a good thing. Feeling the rush of adrenaline and subsequent fear and nervousness is natural and does not mean that you are not equipped to deal with the situation. In fact, the opposite is true. What has made a huge difference to me in high-pressure situations is an acceptance that it is happening to both myself and others in my team and therefore we need to help everyone manage their personal reactions.

- The fight or flight system is not a choice it is a chemical reaction to stress
- Deal with the anxiety before you tackle the problem
- Use intelligence not information to help manage the reaction
- Stressors are specific to individual people.

Relieve pressure

Recently we have created a culture where we increase pressure as a way to force people to try and increase their performance. I believe that we should be relieving and reducing pressure in order to increase the performance of our teams, and therefore enable them to become more effective. Sandstone have been involved with several elite triathletes, including Georgia Taylor Brown and Chantelle Cummings. Georgia, you may have seen, won a silver medal at the Tokyo Olympics in 2021.

If either of their running times were not as fast as they needed to be, in order to win races, their coaches don't tell them that they are not good enough and shout at them to run faster. As elite athletes, they are aware of what is required at the highest level. They are aware of the performances of their nearest competitors. What is required is constructive guidance and tools in our toolkit to increase that performance. Merely pointing out that that split wasn't fast enough does not help us increase performance or find the solution. We see the same in business. We see a situation where the target hasn't been achieved or we're behind a particular performance or curve. We see managers and leaders point out to the team that they are behind the curve, not achieving the required standards and that they need to get on and sell more!

Assuming that we are starting with a high-performance team that has been recruited well in the first place, then that team is well aware that it hasn't made its target and that it is not going to receive a bonus this month. These facts don't need pointing out to them. In fact, it may be true that the added pressure is one of the factors making the team choke and not perform. Simply adding more pressure makes the situation worse, not better.

What we need to do is to create a safe space for the team to operate in. Enable the team to relieve the pressure, to work together and collaborate to find a way to achieve the target. As a leader, try to remember that the aim is to increase performance and move towards the outcome through enabling them to be effective, not to point out their failings! That's not to say that we should lower the targets or that we should settle for a lesser performance. It just means we must understand the outcome and how we achieve it. It stands to reason that if a junior member of your team is making mistakes because they feel as though they're under pressure, adding pressure is only going to see them make more mistakes. They will feel more vulnerable and ultimately this will decrease the team's performance. It is true to say that a little bit of pressure often increases the performance of an individual. Maybe we should switch on that fight or flight mechanism, increase the adrenaline, and focus the mind, but that is very much a little-and-often scenario, not something that's sustainable, and not something that works particularly well in a long-term environment where complex decision-making is required.

I did some work with the members of an elite female football team. One of the strikers kept missing the goal, and just at the key moment of a game. Now, I should reiterate at this moment that I know very little about football therefore it might seem as though I am a strange person to ask. But actually, it's all about communication under pressure and enabling the leadership to become more effective. I was shown video footage of the player constantly missing goals when the big moments arose. I got together with the team and told them that I had a very simple solution. I told them that they needed to drop the player from the team as she was clearly not performing to the required standard.

All her team members instantly leapt to her defence. They told me that they could definitely not do this and explained that she was the best striker they had. I explained that all of the evidence that they had shown me pointed to her lack of performance.

They again assured me that she was the very best player they had and that under normal circumstances she never missed a goal. I asked them to explain what they meant by normal circumstances. The team then proceeded to explain to me that in the build-up to games and, of course, in training, she never missed a goal. She could score with either her left or right foot, from almost anywhere on the pitch. She was pretty much guaranteed to put the ball in the back of the net. I explained that I thought this was strange as all the evidence they had shown did not support this and I asked what had changed. The team then pointed out to me that it was only in the big games, only when the pressure really came on that she struggled to find her form. I asked them what it was they felt changed during these big matches. Of course, they replied that it was the pressure. I summed up that it was when the pressure was increased that she seemed to miss the goal or perform at the level they all knew she was capable of. All agreed. I asked them to watch the video footage they had sent to me again, only this time not to focus on the player trying to put the ball in the back of the net or the positioning of the other players, but rather the reactions of the players after the goal had already been missed. Of course, just like any of us would, and totally understandably, as the ball flashed wide and missed the net, all of the teammates found themselves acting in despair. Hands were raised, heads were shaken, and words of disappointment were voiced.

Of course, none of this was meant to be malicious in any way towards the player who just missed the goal. I then asked if we were to put *ourselves* in the position of the player who had just missed the goal, how would we then feel? Had the pressure been relieved or increased? The answer is that the team had actually and unwittingly increased the pressure on the player. The team had made their disappointment in her performance very clear. They provided no constructive advice as to how we might be able to move forward. In fact, they increased the pressure on the player which we all agreed was the factor that caused the problem in the first place. Together, we worked out a system whereby whenever a player missed a goal, especially if it was early in the game, the team would try doubly hard to reassure her. They would explain that they understood that she was the best person to be in the team and that she was the best chance they had of scoring goals; that they all understood that she would be okay and she would get there. In other words, we made a real attempt to commit to relieving the pressure on the goal taker, rather than adding to it. Once the pressure was relieved, the player was able to relax and cope much better with the pressure. As a result, her goal and her strike rate increased. Reducing the pressure on the player had increased performance.

Whilst on operational tours of duty in Afghanistan and involved in several serious gunfights, I can assure you that no part of me needed to remind our soldiers that they were in a dangerous and stressful situation. The bullets whistling past them gave that away. My job as a leader was to relieve the pressure and provide reassurance and direction to enable the team to deal with the pressure that was on all of us. The same is true in business.

I like to use the analogy of an umbrella. Imagine that your team is standing in the rain, getting wet and cold. The result of being wet and cold is that they can't perform at their best. They become insular, not thinking at the same level they would normally. As one of the stronger team members, I'm going to put up an umbrella; I'm going to create a safe space for the team to operate in. I'm going to create an area, or air gap if you like, where there is no rain. This will enable the team to regain their composure, focus on what they need to do and build a strategy to cope. In other words, I'm going to create space by shielding my team from the pressure. I'll do this for as long as it's needed for them to them step up with a solution to collaborate and become more effective. I have put up the umbrella and sheltered my team.

We often talk about diversity and diversity is an expression that in my view has recently become kidnapped. If I was to stand on stage and say to you that we're going to talk about diversity today. The majority would assume that we were going to talk about race, creed, colour, or sexuality. Of course, all of those things we just mentioned are important. Equally important are different leadership and communication styles and a variety of different personality types. Teams should be able to cover each other's blind spots.

In other words, if there's an area that I'm particularly bad at, it's important that one of my team members is particularly good at that situation. This enables them to be at their best when I'm at my worst and we are covering all the blind spots within the team. This means that different members of the team will feel under pressure at different times and will often react differently to each other in different circumstances. Let me explain: I can be walking along the summit of a mountain and feel relatively cool, calm, and collected.

I'm in a situation that I understand, with people that I trust, and I've trained and prepared for this moment. We finish the expedition and suddenly I'm required to write the post-activity report. I have to provide a spreadsheet to deliver the accounts in order to close the books and demonstrate the expedition finances to the sponsors. I become anxious and nervous. In other words, my fight or flight mechanism has been triggered. Although easy for some, this side of the expedition creates in me the greatest anxiety. It's neither better nor worse, it's just different. At this stage I seek the support of other team members who were perhaps not so strong on the mountain, overcoming their own fear of falling, but who love numbers and are quicky able to create spreadsheets. We have created mutual support for each other in situations that we find challenging.

The point we need to understand here is that all of our team members will feel pressure from different situations and different circumstances. It's important we try not to judge what it is that has triggered the stress reaction, but we acknowledge that it has happened and support as best we can. We should remind ourselves that in this set of circumstances I am strong and able to cope. Therefore, I am going to put up the umbrella and create a safe space in which to operate. In a different set of circumstances, the following day or the following week, it may be my other team member that is actually best placed to put up the umbrella and create a shelter and safe space for me to take advantage of.

A great deal has been written about using psychological profiling as both a recruitment and a team development tool. I have certainly been subjected to various forms of this testing over the years and believe that when used correctly it can be very effective. When we are looking to understand our existing team or put a team together for a particular challenge, we rarely have either the funding or time to conduct a DISC or a Myers-Briggs profile. We can carry out a simple assessment of our team though.

We use four categories:

The Controller: This person likes to be in charge and take control of a situation. They are task-orientated and get things done, often effective in a high-pressure or time critical situation, and less interested in details and planning and would rather get on with the task. They are often self-assured and forthcoming with their views. They may have a high tolerance for risk.

The Entertainer: This person is charismatic and often humorous. They can provide a team with morale and motivation, they may be seen by others as shallow or loud, and they are often quick thinkers and need an audience to be at their best.

The Thinker: This person is methodical and effective. They will work out every detail and often do not like to be rushed, are effective problem solvers but often require space and time to be at their best, and they are excellent project managers and planners but less effective in time-sensitive situations.

The Feeler: This person is genuinely motivated by the team and being a part of the collective. They are excellent team members and will be aware of all the politics and tensions within a team and they can appear indecisive and may find it difficult to take tough decisions.

Most people are a mix of these personality types but for the purposes of this exercise it is easier to view a person's primary characteristics. In an ideal team we would have a mix of these personality types. This gives the team flexibility and means that whatever the task, we should always have a team member who is strong.

You can get a great understanding of your team by completing a simple exercise. Make two lists under the following headings:

- List of your team members
- Skills / attributes required to face the challenge or situation.

Using the list of each of your team members, write next to their names which of the four personality types you think they are. Then add a list of their skills or experiences. You should now be able to make a note of what type of situation they are likely to perform well in and what type of situation they are likely to find most challenging.

For the second list, make a note of the scenarios that you think you might face. For each scenario make a note of the personality type best suited to that scenario then add a list of the skills you think will be required.

You should now be able to cross-reference the two lists. You can match the names of the team members to the scenarios and situations that you might face. This will enable you to select the right person for the right job at the right time.

Finally, you should be able to add a third column which contains the personalities and skills that may be missing from the team. These can be addressed via training or recruitment.

So far in this section of the book we've looked at false expectations appearing real. We've looked at the fight or flight mechanism and how it's a biological and chemical reaction to circumstances around us, not a choice. We've discussed the idea of relieving pressure, not adding pressure, in order to get our team to perform to the best of its abilities.

It's now possible to see how all three of these elements add together to create analysis paralysis and stop us being as effective as we want to be. The perception of pressure increases which in turn leads to false expectation. We start to worry about the things that could, might, or should happen. We contemplate consequences that aren't actually real and we start to move down a catastrophic thinking cycle. This triggers our fight or flight mechanism that essentially narrows our vision, makes us more aggressive, and prepares us to fight or to run away. This combination of events in turn stops us being able to react in the most cognitive or effective way just at the moment when we most need to.

Whilst leading a group of experienced skiers in the wild mountain resort of La Grave in France, one member of my group became paralysed by fear. This is not a criticism but merely an observation. The slope had become steeper, and the snow had thickened and become more difficult to ski in. This, combined with a perception of the ice towering above us, triggered the fight or flight mechanism. The false expectation or FEAR then started to take place. The skier suddenly started to believe that she had no way out of this situation. She believed that wasn't up to it and wouldn't make it down the mountain. She was creating self-imposed pressure which in turn was confirming the body's fight or flight mechanism and heightening her sense of fear. This was leading to yet more catastrophic thinking. You don't need to be a ski instructor to understand that in this set of circumstances, telling somebody to calm down is not very useful. I'm sure we've all been told to calm down at some point and I'm sure we're all aware of the effect that had on us.

The other factor to consider is that in this scenario on the side of a glacier in La Grave there was no other way down, no alternative route. As a leader and teammate, you have to think about how you can relieve pressure. How can you enable this person to be the best that they can be right now, in order to get them down the side of the mountain? Being able to keep the rest of the group safe and get them down the mountain is also dependent on our ability to relieve pressure and to increase the performance of this individual.

In this situation, the first thing we did was understand that the fight or flight mechanism was very real for this individual. The fear and subsequent anxiety were causing the paralysis. The first thing we must do is take a moment. We suggested that she remove her goggles, take off her helmet, and sit down in the snow. She took a drink and a few deep breaths. This allowed the chemicals that were rushing around her body to dissipate a little and increased the oxygen flow to the brain, which in turn allowed her pulse rate to come back down again. Once this has been achieved, she is now much more open and responsive to any suggestions that I might be able to make. It would have been very easy at this stage to point out the consequences of her actions and tell her that the rest of the group was dependent on her in order to get off the side of this mountain and remind her that there was no alternative.

However, all those statements, whilst true, are not necessarily enabling me to achieve my outcome, which is to build this person's confidence back up again and release them from the FEAR. Then of course I need to achieve the aim of removing the entire group safely, and ideally with some fun to the bottom of the mountain. What I did in this situation was point out all the things that this person had done well: we were halfway down the mountain and we had already skied some of the steepest, most challenging terrain on the mountain. I quietly and confidently pointed out that she had, in fact, already achieved many of the things that she was afraid of. Her technique had already supported her this far. I reminded her that, up to this point, she had skied like one of the strongest members of the group.

#BecauseICan – La Grave

La Grave is a small ski resort in the French alps dominated by the mountain La Meije. The area is not prepared and, although patrolled, has no formal avalanche control. The area is dangerous to ski unless supported by a guide, including much glacier travel at the very top. La Grave is visited by off-piste and extreme skiers. The vertical drop totals 2,150 m. Although it is possible to ski below the resort to the road and increase the vertical descent to 2,300 m, mechanical access to the mountain is limited.

The other group members also demonstrated a touch of vulnerability. They also pointed out that they were nervous, outside of their comfort zone, and having to concentrate exceedingly hard on making their turns and managing the terrain. This touch of vulnerability ensured that our skier didn't feel alone and instead felt part of the team. She was reassured that she wasn't simply the weakest link in the team. The next thing to do was to create a contract or an agreement as to what we could achieve. Rather than focus on the whole mountain, the steep terrain, or the hour and a half or so of skiing that was still in front of us, we broke everything down into smaller sections. We asked the skier to look ahead of us and to identify a plateau section of the mountain that was flat, comfortable, and that she felt that she could get to. So, together we planned a route to that section. We asked one of the other members of the group to ski there first to prove that it was possible, thus alleviating any fear or false expectation. Then together we skied the 60 metres to the plateau. Being able to do that then meant that the fight or flight mechanism started to abate, and confidence again started to build. Relieving the pressure had enabled this individual to resort back to the excellent technique and confidence that had got her this far down the mountain. We simply then repeated the process as we went. As the confidence grew, the performance came back. The level of support required was reduced and the legs between stops got bigger, until eventually, an hour or so later, we all found ourselves at the bottom of the mountain, ordering a beer.

I like to use this type of example, because in such a situation it wouldn't occur to anybody to increase the pressure on the person who was afraid on the side of a mountain. When we find ourselves in a high-pressure situation but in a softer environment, we are often dealing with all of the same reactions and behaviours and yet, for some reason, we often increase pressure to reiterate that targets aren't being met. We remind the person that they need to perform if they want to keep their job. It's important that we focus on the outcome and remember that the outcome is to get this person operating back to the very best of their ability. Remind yourself that this person was a valued member of the team, that they were recruited for a reason, and normally they are good at their job. Then focus on what it is that's causing the anxiety and the pressure and relieve that pressure: find small steps to enable that person to make progress. Once they're making progress, build upon or reward the behaviours that you want to see again.

So what?

Relieving pressure, no matter how slight, can break the cycle of catastrophic thinking and prevent analysis paralysis. Look to support team members and ensure everybody understands the value that each brings to the challenge. The more diverse the team and its skill sets, the more likely it is to be able to deal with a multitude of challenges and situations. It can prove challenging to surround yourself with people who have different personality types or characteristics to yourself but the benefits far outweigh the downsides. Remember that you might have to work harder to communicate with someone of a different personality type. Your mother may have told you to treat people the way you would like to be treated. This is not true! Treat them the way *they* would like to be treated.

- Cover each other's blind spots
- Relieve pressure to increase performance
- Create a safe space for the team to operate in
- You lead people and manage numbers.

Part 4

BUILD RESILIENCE BY EXPLAINING THE "IN ORDER TO..."

In this part of the book, we will look in depth at how important it is to understand why you are doing something. We will utilize the British Military "in order to" system to implement this.

Why are we doing this?

The single biggest key to unlocking your ability to be effective and to achieve the mission is to understand your why. In order to avoid simply going through the motions and ticking boxes, your team must understand its purpose: it is about not only what it is trying to achieve but why. Understanding your "in order to" can transform not only an individual performance, but also that of your team.

Whether you're in a leadership role, looking to motivate yourself to achieve that first 5k run, or climb a mountain, understanding why you are doing something, and what it is that you are trying to achieve, will be one of the most enabling concepts that you can adopt. The former team GB cycling coach David Brailsford, of marginal gains fame, once explained that when an athlete enters a four-year Olympic cycle it is totally understandable that their motivation will ebb and flow. They will have days when they leap out of bed and can't wait to get to the velodrome or the gym. They will have other days when they're tired, it's raining outside, and it's too early in the morning. The thought of training again today doesn't appeal. This is completely normal and something we will talk about later. Brailsford then goes on to explain that it is okay for motivation to ebb and flow but what should be unrelenting is the commitment. If you understand your beliefs and motivations, if you understand why it is that you are trying to achieve something, then finding the motivation or enabling yourself to push through some of the more tedious tasks you're asked to perform becomes that little bit easier. Whenever you set out on a major project, whether that's attempting to climb Mount Everest, riding the Dakar Rally, or getting promoted at work, it is almost inevitable that the path that you follow will change.

#BecauseICan – Marginal Gains

On taking over as the head of Team GB cycling, Sir David Brailsford implemented a policy of seeking marginal gains. The whole principle came from the idea that if you broke down everything you could think of that goes into riding a bike and then improved it by 1%, you will get a significant increase when you put them all together. There's fitness and conditioning, of course, but there are other things that might seem on the periphery, like sleeping in the right position, having the same pillow when you are away and training in different places. They're tiny things but if you clump them together it makes a big difference. The result is continuous improvement at every level. During the Olympic games in London the team won 12 medals, eight of which were gold.

Focusing on the bigger picture and why you are carrying out a particular task can provide personal and team motivation. That cold, wet run on a Saturday morning can be soul-destroying and feel pointless. Focusing on that run as part of the process that will make your first marathon a success and help you raise sponsorship for your chosen charity can be uplifting.

The same is true when we are looking to empower our teammates. The "in order to" was first taught to me whilst attending the Royal Military Academy at

Sandhurst. As you can imagine, as well as polishing shoes, learning to do drill, and fitness, a huge amount of time is spent on learning to understand motivation, inspiration, and how to lead people in high-pressure environments.

Essentially, rather than simply telling someone to perform a particular task, we should always explain why that task needs performing and what its place is within the bigger picture.

We were taught that the key to this was being able to deliver an "in order to". Let me explain: rather than simply say to you, "I want you to go and do this task...", what I'm going to say to you is, "I want you to go and do this in order that we can achieve this...".

Ask yourself: how many times have you been micromanaged? How many times during your career have you been simply told to go and perform a task, seemingly thanklessly and blindly? Did it leave you feeling motivated, enthused, and focused on achieving the very best outcome that you possibly could? Or did you find yourself frustrated, head down, and lacking purpose?

There are times when we are just simply required to get the job done, to perform a task, or to see something through for the sake of doing it. As somebody looking to inspire and empower our teammates, it's important that we understand that whilst occasionally we may just need a job done, micromanaging provides none of the things we've just discussed. In fact, the opposite, it will demotivate, disempower, and often cost us more time.

When we're the expert in a particular field, it's easy for us to micromanage. We give out tasks blindly and provide corrections when the team has not been performing to the level that we felt they should have. The reason for this is that you've been performing this task for 20 years and the person who's new to the role has been performing that task for maybe a few months, possibly even less. Therefore, by definition, you are better at it than they are. When they come to you with a problem, or they're unable to focus or deliver the result that you want, you simply step in. You micromanage and you correct or "red pen" their work before going back to doing what you were doing before. What you've just done is halted the learning and development of that individual. You have devalued that member of your team.

We can stop this happening by delivering the "in order to". At Sandhurst we would often be given the role of the platoon commander, the officer commanding up to 30 soldiers. As the course progressed across 12 months, we would be set more and more complex missions. We would be expected to plan the outcomes and to work out what aims we were trying to achieve, and then to brief and direct our soldiers towards achieving that outcome.

As an officer, I would say to my soldiers, "I need you to capture the bridge across the river in order that we can get the supplies across the river to the other side and support the soldiers that are further up the valley who need our help". Those soldiers then go down to the river, and they find that the bridge is heavily defended, much more defended than the intelligence had told us. The problem of taking the bridge is going to be significantly more challenging, take more time, and possibly incur losses that we are not prepared to take. Because we've delivered the *in order to*, the soldiers are then empowered to think for themselves.

The *in order to* was to get the supplies across the river to support the soldiers further up the valley. The soldiers then don't need to ask permission to change the plan. They know what it is that they need to achieve, and they're empowered to take their own initiative. They search left and right along the river and find an alternative crossing where the river shallows and is relatively unguarded. Without having to refer to the officers, or the sergeants, the team moves to the shallow crossing point, secures it, and allows the supplies to cross the river. They can assist those soldiers further up the valley that require their support. The relatively simple act of explaining to the soldiers why and what it was that we were trying to achieve enabled them to think for themselves. It provided them with the freedom of thought to carry out that particular action. In this example, had we not delivered the *in order to*, those soldiers would have come back to the command post and explained that they couldn't take the bridge.

The command team would have gone back down to look for themselves and the planning process would have to start again, all of which is taking up time and resources. The whole process would have gone back into a reverse cycle before a different plan could be configured and tried again. Always ensure that your team members and your colleagues understand the outcome that it is you're trying to achieve, and understand why it is that you're doing something. This will empower them and enable them to seek out solutions.

Rather than coming back to you with what they can't do and what won't work, they are now individually empowered to become part of the solution. If you find yourself in a situation where your team members or colleagues are continually telling you what won't work and what they can't do, my suggestion is that they don't have an *in order to*. They don't understand why they have been asked to perform a particular task, and they are not sufficiently empowered to find the solution. This is, in fact, often a leadership problem, not a decision-making problem.

Some of the tasks that we were set were almost impossible to achieve. We were deliberately fed complex, misleading, or incomplete information from which we were supposed to do our planning. In other words, the chances of us coming up with a fool-proof plan based on the intelligence that we were being given was almost none.

The officers weren't able to provide the guidance because this wasn't in the plan. The *in order to* is what enables us to empower the team to maintain momentum and to deal with the problem in front of us, whilst working towards achieving the outcome, even if the plan and the process changes.

#BecuseICan – Army Officer Commissioning Course

All potential army officers are trained at the Royal Military Academy Sandhurst. The Academy's stated aim is to be "the national centre of excellence for leadership". All British Army officers, including late-entry officers who were previously Warrant Officers, as well as other men and women from overseas, are trained at The Academy. Sandhurst develops leadership in cadets by expanding their character, intellect and professional competences to a level demanded of an Army Officer on first appointment through military training and education. There are three commissioning courses run at the academy. All are accredited by various academic and professional institutions, in particular the Chartered Management Institute. The Regular Commissioning Course lasts for 44 weeks for Direct Entry officers into the Regular service.

It's been widely reported that the current generation are difficult to manage, that they're entitled and want to be part of the big picture, that they need to be contributing and have a purpose to everything that they're doing. As a result, they've been described as difficult to manage and difficult to lead. This is challenging for more senior and older members of the team. Those of us that are a little older have, in fact, created the problem. The current generation require leading and motivating, not managing. In recent years, we've developed a culture where we attempt to lead people with spreadsheets, graphs, and KPIs, whereas, in fact, what we should be doing is delivering an *in order to*. Simply micromanaging people demotivates them. It's possible that my generation potentially put up with too much and allowed this to happen. Whilst delivering an *in order to* can't make those menial tasks any more interesting or guarantee a bigger role in the business, what it does do is help the individual to understand that whilst this particular task may be tedious and not what they signed up to do when they went to university, it is nonetheless vital to achieving the bigger picture. In other words, that menial task plays a key function as part of the bigger *in order to*. By understanding this, the individual is now more empowered and understands their role. This, in turn, creates motivation, empowerment, and enables people to get the job done.

Perhaps the most famous example of this is when President Kennedy was visiting the American space programme. He'd spent many hours meeting the astronauts, scientists, training team, and the controllers. On leaving the building, he walked across the vast hangar where the spacecraft were constructed and stored. In the corner was the janitor sweeping up the floor. President Kennedy turned to the janitor and said that he thought his job must be to keep everything clean and tidy? Without so much as a hesitation the janitor turned to the President and replied absolutely not. He explained that his job was to help put a man on the moon. In other words, although his task was that of sweeping the floor, his *in order to* was to put a man on the moon.

So what?

Every expedition, challenge, or project that I have taken on has required far more menial, planning, and logistical support than the headline tasks of climbing or riding the event. As you have probably gathered from this book, I am not one for menial detailed tasks and struggle to see them through. As a result, the ability to empower others, help them see the bigger picture, and how it relates to them has been a critical skill to develop.

- Always deliver an *in order to* when briefing your team
- Empower by helping the team understand their part in the big picture
- Enable the team to be part of the solution
- Never micromanage.

Enable resilience

Resilience is a subject or a quality that has become an exceedingly hot topic and has been talked about greatly over the last few years. One of the misnomers surrounding resilience is it is in some way a qualification or a course that you can go on. People are often described as being resilient. I believe that you become resilient over a period of time and through training, collaboration, practice and enabling, and communicating effectively, your ability to become more resilient improves. There will be times in your life where you are more resilient than others. We mentioned David Brailsford earlier, who believes that your motivation will ebb and flow, but provided that your commitment to the goal remains constant, then you will achieve your ultimate goal. Resilience can be described in much the same way. We have all experienced days where we feel as though we can take on the world, nothing is in our way, no goal is too hard for us to achieve. Then, for seemingly no apparent reason, we have other days where we don't want to get out of bed in the morning. We can't see a way through, there is no light at the end of the tunnel.

Probably one of the most common questions I've ever asked when doing after-dinner speaking is, do I ever want to quit? Did I ever want to give up? The answer to that is, of course, yes. On every single one of the challenges that I've undertaken, be them physical, mental, or even those faced trying to run our business through troubled waters during the global pandemic, I have thought about giving up. Several times a week, I find myself thinking that I can't go on, that I don't want to do this anymore.

What makes us different is resilience, our ability to not quit. So, the first thing to take away from this is just because you doubt yourself, or you have thoughts of not wanting to continue or wanting to give up, doesn't mean you're not resilient. Angela Duckworth, in her book *Grit*, talks about grit and resilience being probably the single most important factor as to whether we achieve success or not. She conducted studies at West Point, the American Army Officer training centre. She found that rather than any single characteristic, whether physical or mental, indicating their chances of success, the overriding indicator was whether a person was able to demonstrate grit. Grit seriously increased their chances to pass the arduous selection process and become officers. Chris Archer, the famous American baseball player, once explained that it had taken him ten years to become an overnight success. What I take from this, therefore, is that in fact it is resilience that enables us to achieve our goals. If resilience is not a course or a qualification, how do we set the conditions for success? How do we develop resilience that enables us as individuals to initially motivate our fellow teammates to become more resilient, and to enable resilience within ourselves when we're having those days where we can't see a way forward?

For the next section of this book, I want you to imagine that you have woken up one morning and you've decided to climb Mount Everest. You've done very little mountaineering before, but you're determined to stand on the highest point on Earth. You've done all the things that we spoke about so far in this book. You've worked out who you need to collaborate with, done your intelligence not your information, you've got a plan, a training programme, and you've got the right team around you. You now spend the best part of two years raising funds and training. At this stage, even getting to the foot of the mountain seems like a long way away. Every spare minute of the day is spent planning, training, communicating, and focusing on one goal: getting to the foot of Mount Everest.

As time marches on, the funding falls into place, the correct permissions and permits to climb arrive, and you're finally almost there. You spend two weeks at Leeds University locked in a small room with all the air taken out of it, simulating high altitude, preparing yourself for the rigours of the mountain. You eventually find yourself at Heathrow Airport with your teammates and Sky News. The excitement and the adrenaline build. You land in Nepal and make your way via some of the most hair-raising roads you can ever come across to the Tibetan side of the mountain. As a team, you've decided that you're going to conquer the route first explored by Mallory: the northern side of the mountain. It is less popular, and some would say more challenging than the more traditional southern route favoured by the majority of high-altitude mountaineers. As you eventually arrive across the Tibetan plains, at the foot of Mount Everest, you get your first look at the biggest mountain in the world.

This is both exhilarating and intimidating at the same time. Part of you wants to turn around and go home. Part of you thinks it is just too big a mission to achieve, whilst the other part of you can't wait to set foot on the mountain. What you do know is that for the last two years you have spent every waking hour preparing to arrive at this single moment. You are prepared, you are with the right people, and you're ready to go. At this point, your head Sherpa turns to you and explains that what you need to do now is nothing! In fact, you need to sit and rest for an extended period of time, imagine the frustration. You think to yourself, "I'm ready to go. I'm trained, I'm fit, I'm strong, we've got the right equipment. I want to get on and I want to do this". But no, you follow the advice, you sit, looking at the mountain. Eventually the day comes when you first get to set foot on the mountain.

With your equipment all packed and your guides with you, you set off towards advanced base camp (ABC) on the northern side of the mountain. Three or four hours of trekking at high altitude see you arrive at ABC. Again, you stop, rest, spend the night. In the morning, you head back down the mountain. This perhaps is not what you'd envisaged. It's not what you thought was going to happen. Why am I going back down the mountain when I came here to climb to the highest point on Earth? In fact, this process continues. You climb from one camp to the next then rest, spend the night and come back down again. Sometimes you even come back down all the way to base camp for an extended period of time, resting and acclimatizing before yet again setting out to walk along the path that you've already been along but climbing higher this time. As you do so, you question yourself more and more. Why am I here? What's going on? What is this all about? I don't understand. Why am I coming down to go back up? Why are we following this circular route when I can see the summit of the mountain, and all I want to do is crack on? Why have I spent two years of my life training for this? Why have I put every penny that I've got into finding a way to make this expedition happen? All these doubts start to creep into your mind and make you question why you're there and whether you even want to continue with this expedition.

As we've discussed earlier in this book, we're beginning to set up a series of catastrophic thoughts. Okay, that's the worst-case scenario. So, let's step out of this situation for a minute and look at how we can create better resilience. Let's look at how we can create circumstances where we might be able to enable better resilience within our teammates. What I've just described to you, whilst physically is what happens whilst climbing a mountain, from a communication and a psychological point of view, is not what we did.

Let me explain. Before going to Everest, we received a series of lectures from our friends at Leeds University and from other experienced, high-altitude mountaineers. Our team doctor Kirstie explained to us the intricacies of what goes on in the human body as we climb higher and higher. I certainly don't claim to be a biologist, but in layman's terms, this is what happens. As we climb up the mountain, the air becomes thinner. There is less oxygen for the body to take in. Therefore, we struggle to operate at our usual capacity. I'm sure if you've seen the movies, you will have heard of the expression, the death zone. This is the area in which the human body is fundamentally dying, and despite the myths, no human being can survive at these altitudes for extended periods of time. When we climb into higher altitudes, the body does its best to adapt to what's going on around us. Our spleen will secrete more red blood cells into our blood supply. Those red blood cells enable us to carry more oxygen. Our ability to carry more oxygen means that we can harvest more oxygen from the thinner air around us, and thus enable us to perform better at these higher altitudes. As we come back down the mountain the air begins to thicken, and as we come lower the oxygen density increases. Our body is able to recover and to rest better at the lower altitudes. We then manufacture more red blood cells. This further increases our ability to carry oxygen. The adaptation and recovery take place more effectively whilst we come lower and rest up. This process is often called acclimatization. The medical team then explained that the slower we climb the mountain, the greater our chances of success. This is because we are giving our body the best possible opportunity to acclimatize to the altitude. In fact, every time we rest up, turn around, and come back down again, we are increasing our chances of success for reaching the summit. One of the common factors often not discussed around climbing mountains the size of Mount Everest is the fact that the summit is only halfway. Sadly, a number of climbers perish or get into difficulty on their way back down the mountain. This is because they've paid too high a price, physiologically, on the way up the mountain, and are unable to complete the second half of the journey from the summit, back to base camp.

Every time we turnaround, take our time and allow our bodies to acclimatize, the greater are our chances not only of reaching the summit, but of returning safely to Basecamp. Now, when we're on the side of the mountain, and we're thinking to ourselves, why are we turning round, why are we coming back down again, rather than the catastrophic thinking spiral setting in and us questioning why we're there, we now understand that we're part of the solution. As a team member, I now understand that every time I turn around, or rest, I am in fact increasing my chances of reaching the top of the mountain, and more importantly, coming back down safely. The mountain hasn't become any shorter, the winds haven't got any less ferocious, and it's certainly no warmer. What has changed is that we've understood our 'in order to'. We've understood that we are part of the solution. So, although we're performing this seemingly meaningless task of going down the mountain when, in fact, we want to climb to reach the summit, we now understand this is all part of the process which will enable success.

This simple change of communication, education, and effective collaboration with the medical team has meant that we have enabled resilience.

By understanding the why and ensuring that the team members around us understand the purpose of our actions, we are all able to look after and support each other. We can remind our teammates that although this might be a bit tedious today, having to go back down the mountain to come back up again, we are, in fact, creating a situation to enable us to succeed. In other words, we are becoming resilient.

For our team on the side of Mount Everest in 2015, the outcome did not end the way we had all hoped. In fact, the largest earthquakes, and subsequent avalanches, ever to hit the Nepalese and Tibetan region struck. Many thousands of people were killed across the mountainous regions and back in Kathmandu. Several hundred climbers and expeditions perished on the side of the mountain that day in 2015.

#BecauseICan – Mount Everest

Mount Everest is the highest mountain above sea level on Earth. It stands at 8,848 m tall. Mount Everest attracts many climbers, including highly experienced mountaineers. There are two main climbing routes, one approaching the summit from the southeast in Nepal (known as the "standard route") and the other from the north in Tibet. While not posing substantial technical climbing challenges on the standard route, Everest presents dangers such as altitude sickness, weather and wind, as well as significant hazards from avalanches and the Khumbu Icefall. As of 2019, over 300 people have died on Everest: many of whose bodies remain on the mountain. The first recorded efforts to reach Everest's summit were made by British mountaineers. As Nepal did not allow foreigners to enter the country at the time, the British made several attempts on the north ridge route from the Tibetan side. After the first reconnaissance expedition by the British in 1921 reached 7,000 m on the North Col, the 1922 expedition pushed the north ridge route up to 8,320 m, marking the first time a human had climbed above 8,000 m. The 1924 expedition resulted in one of the greatest mysteries on Everest to this day: George Mallory and Andrew Irvine made a final summit attempt on 8 June but never returned, sparking debate as to whether or not they were the first to reach the top. Tenzing Norgay and Edmund Hillary made the first official ascent of Everest in 1953, using the southeast ridge route.

During the afternoon of 25 April 2015, an earthquake measuring 7.8 struck Nepal and surrounding countries. Shaking from the quake triggered an avalanche from Pumori into Base

Camp on Mount Everest. It is believed 22 people were killed, making it the deadliest disaster on the mountain, surpassing an avalanche that occurred in 2014. Many thousands were killed in the surrounding towns and villages.

You might be asking yourself, how does climbing on the side of the world's biggest mountain relate to me at home or in a business environment? Let me help you translate. Whilst often we set out to achieve the headline goal, the glamorous job or the big target, achieving that will require us to perform several menial tasks. We will fail on a number of occasions and get told "no" more than we get told "yes". We may be required to change course or change direction on several occasions. Just like us on the side of the mountain you will find yourself having to come back down in order to go back up. As a team, if you can explain to yourselves before you kick off that there are going to be a number of menial tasks that we need to perform that are going to be boring, it is highly likely before we get told yes, we're going to get told no on a number of occasions.

Your team, whilst they won't necessarily enjoy the long menial task or the long hours, will all understand that this is part of the bigger picture and a vital step in the process to achieving success. In other words, you are allowing them to become resilient. You are setting the circumstances for success and enabling them to cope and accept the more tedious and challenging roles that are required before achieving overall success.

So what?

Nobody is born resilient. The next time that you doubt yourself or consider giving up, remember that those thoughts are totally normal and to be expected. The same is true of your teammates. Expect them to question what they are doing and their motivation. Be prepared to explain the "in order to" and empower them wherever possible.

- We become resilient over time
- Set expectation levels
- Create the circumstances where success is possible
- Utilize the "why" to enable resilience.

Avoid the dangerous middle ground

I find one of the biggest challenges faced when trying to implement advice or guidance from friends and colleagues or even self-help books like this one is that when we are sitting in the comfort of our own home, relaxed and not under any pressure, the advice seems so simple and easy to implement. When we most need that advice is usually in the opposite of the situation in which we're often given it. We find ourselves anxious, under pressure, tired and perhaps unable to see a way forward. As a long-term sufferer of depression and anxiety, I often find one of the most challenging circumstances is when I can feel myself becoming more anxious and I can feel the dark clouds rolling in. I know I'm beginning to react in a way that is not my normal response to any given situation. This is the moment at which all that advice and guidance is the most difficult to implement, and yet the moment at which we most need it. In 2018, the directors of Sandstone decided that we were going to undertake a year of challenges. We wanted to inspire and motivate as many people as possible under the hashtag, Because I Can (#BecauseICan). We wanted people to pick a challenge, push themselves just a little bit further than they would normally go and discover something about themselves and in the process discover coping strategies and lessons that they could then take away and implement into their everyday family and business lives. In order to practice what we preach, we undertook a challenge once a month, every month for an entire year. Those challenges saw us doing things such as 70.3 Ironman triathlons, The Three Peaks challenge, and L'Etape du Tour... more of this shortly.

#BecauseICan – The Three Peaks Challenge

The National Three Peaks Challenge involves climbing the three highest peaks of Scotland, England and Wales, often within 24 hours. The total walking distance is 23 miles (37 km) and the total ascent is 3,064 metres. The total driving distance is 462 miles. The three mountains are Snowdon in Wales (1,085 m), Scafell Pike in England (978m) and Ben Nevis in Scotland (1,345 m). A popular misconception is that the three mountains that form the challenge are the three tallest on the British mainland. Rather, they are the tallest mountains within each representative country: Scafell Pike is the tallest in England, Snowdon is the tallest in Wales and Ben Nevis the tallest in Scotland — over 100 peaks in Scotland are higher than Scafell Pike, and 56 are higher than Snowdon.

The year of challenges provided a second agenda for me. We're often told that when in stressful, high-pressure situations, we need to take time out to calm ourselves down, and to be in the moment. Whilst I certainly wouldn't contradict this advice, if it works for you, unfortunately it doesn't work for me. My mind is often racing and overactive. Some of my most stressful moments are those when I find myself alone with my own thoughts and nothing to preoccupy myself. In fact, riding motorcycles off-road or flying helicopters are some of my most relaxing moments, as my brain is so engaged in complex tasks that all the other dark thoughts move to one side. As a result of this, it may surprise you to know that long endurance challenges pose some of the most difficult situations for me.

Whilst managing the physicality of a given challenge is always difficult, managing the psychological distress that this puts me under raises a far greater challenge. I wanted to spend this year of challenges working out coping strategies and mechanisms that I could use and share with other people, to help push away the dark clouds. When I felt the negative thoughts or the anxiety starting to roll in, what systems, processes, or, more importantly, tools could I put in my toolkit that would enable me to deal better with these situations? One of the challenges that we were going to undertake was a cycling event called L'Etape du Tour. At some point, most of us have watched one of the major cycle races on television, with the Tour de France probably being the most famous. We see these incredible endurance athletes cycling hundreds of kilometres a day at speeds more than 55 kph (kilometres per hour) for three weeks, in the process climbing some of the biggest mountain ranges in France. The level of endurance, fitness, and the ability to endure suffering are almost incomprehensible by the average cyclist, let alone member of the public. L'Etape du Tour is run by the same company, ASO, that run the Tour de France and the Dakar Rally. The event provides amateur cyclists with the opportunity to pit themselves against one of the mountain stages of the Tour de France.

At least one person reading this book has a bicycle that costs more than their car, and probably spends more time than they care to admit to wearing Lycra. If this is you, the L'Etape is the challenge that you should be setting yourself. The organizers of the Tour de France pick one of the high-altitude mountain stages of the tour and open it up to amateur cyclists. Approximately one week later, the pro-peloton rides the same stage! You'll start and finish in the same place as the pro-peloton will race.

#BecauseICan – The Tour de France

The Tour de France is an annual multiple-stage bicycle race primarily held in France, while also occasionally passing through nearby countries. It consists of 21 stages, each a day long, over the course of 23 days. The race was first organized in 1903 to increase sales for the newspaper L'Auto and is currently run by the Amaury Sport Organisation. The race has been held annually since its first edition in 1903 except when it was stopped for the two World Wars. As the Tour gained prominence and popularity, the race was lengthened and its reach began to extend around the globe. Participation expanded from a primarily French field as more riders from all over the world began to participate in the race each year. The Tour is a UCI World Tour event, which means that the teams that compete in the race are mostly UCI World Teams, with the exception of the teams that the organizers invite. It has become "the world's biggest annual sporting event". The riders will cycle in the region of 3,500 km.

On a warm, sunny day in July, I found myself on the start line for L'Etape 2018. We were going to ride from Lake Annecy to Le Grand Bornand in the south of France, covering 169 kilometres with four major climbs on the route: three category one climbs and one HC (or hard climb). As an amusing fact, I discovered much later that a category one climb means that the old French car, the Citron 2CV, would have to engage first gear in order to make it up the hill. The HC category climb means that, in the same car, the occupants would in fact have to get out and push the car to the top of the hill. Prior to the event I thought I was prepared. After all, I had completed a whole series of endurance events throughout the year. As it turns out, I wasn't! I'd received a whole load of advice from friends that had done it before and, of course naturally, from several of the triathletes that we've supported over the years.

The key piece of advice seemed to be, take your time, don't start off too fast. Whatever you do, don't stop. As we set off down the side of Lake Annecy, the excitement and tension were palpable. A total of 15,000 amateur cyclists had decided to push themselves against the mountain stage that day. Early on I found myself going backwards with these incredibly professional-looking cyclists whizzing past me down the side of the lake. I glanced down, and I was still doing 35 kph faster than I would usually like to be cycling. I reassured myself that everything was going to be okay and all I had to do was to keep going.

As we approached the first climb at around the 40 km mark, I settled myself in and mentally prepared myself for the inevitable suffering that was coming. The climb was 12 km in length. It would see us climb from 600 m to 1,470 m above sea level. I had never cycled anything like this before in my life and this was the first of four climbs in the day. I suddenly found myself spiralling out of control. Not literally, but psychologically. As I struggled up this first hill all I could think about was that I stood no chance of completing this course. The voice in my head kept saying "I can't get to the end of this, I've bitten off more than I can chew. I'm not ready for this". I was also really worried about letting down my friends and about admitting failure or going back and telling people that I hadn't succeeded.

For the first time in my life, I felt as though I was just going to fail and I was going to have to accept that. This was still only the first climb of the day. It was at this point that I promised myself that what I was going to do was climb the first hill, no matter what happened, and come down the other side of it. I struggled to the top of the very first hill and paused on the top. I drank some water and consoled myself with the fact that the next bit of this section was downhill. As we started to descend, of course, everything started to feel better. We were descending from approximately the 54 km mark to around the 75 km mark. We then rolled to the base of the next hill. All of a sudden, the imposter syndrome, the fear of failure, and the physical exhaustion kicked back in again. There was no way I was going to be able to complete this challenge. I didn't have it in me, I didn't have it in my legs. And simply, I'd underprepared and not taken this challenge seriously enough. I started to fail, and I started to talk myself out of finishing. I started to convince myself quitting was ok with all sorts of reasons as to why it would be okay for me to quit, and why failure was going to be acceptable.

In a moment of clarity, I stopped myself thinking about the bigger picture. I told myself, all I needed to do was to concentrate on getting to the next checkpoint, nothing else mattered. This is like a pitstop in car racing. It's somewhere you can pull in on your bike, get something to eat, get some water and take a rest. For the moment, all I needed to do was make that food station. I focused on making that individual food station, and I did. Once I got to that station the same thing occurred. I had some food, some water, and told myself I could get to the next water point, which was another 5 km away. In other words, I was now no longer focusing on the large hills or the big distances still to cover.

Merely setting myself smaller and smaller targets enabled me to keep myself moving. I reminded myself that I was doing this challenge to inspire as many people as possible and, hopefully, to motivate a few people that suffered in the same way that I did to have a go and challenge themselves. Therefore, it wasn't okay to quit. I ignored the next two hills and told myself all I needed to do was to get to the next food station. Of course, as fatigue was setting in the challenge was becoming physically more difficult. All I did then was bring my micro goals closer and closer towards myself. In fact, for quite a long time after the cycle I was able to tell you exactly how many lamp posts were at the side of the road on the third climb of the event up a mountain Col de Romme. This was because the only way that I could succeed was to focus on the next lamp post. As I cycled past one lamp post, I would tell myself, I'm just going to get to the next lamp post. As I achieved that lamp post, I would move to the next lamp post and so on.

So, I was quite literally moving one lamp post at a time towards my goal. Having taken on some food, water, and received a little support from social media, I started to feel a little bit stronger. We were now over the 150 km mark and the end was in sight. So now, rather than every single lamp post I started to count out ten lamp posts at a time. Then a kilometre at a time and then the next blind crest on the hill at a time and finally the next summit. I continued this process all the way to the final climb and down to the finish line on the other side. It was probably the longest 10 hours of my life. Without question this was the first time in my life I had ever really doubted my ability to finish the challenge. Therefore, it was important for me to break this down, and to understand what had worked for me and what hadn't worked for me in terms of getting through this challenge. Could I find a way to articulate this in order to share it with other people? The theory that I've come up with is that you must focus on the big picture, ignore the dangerous middle ground, and take small steps towards your goal.

So let me explain. The big picture was the overall ambition, it was my why or my in order to. Why did I get out of bed that morning? Well, I set myself a challenge and it was important to me to inspire as many people as possible. Quitting halfway through the challenge was unlikely to inspire many people and, in fact, may even provide the evidence for a few people that they should never take on this type of challenge. This was certainly not what I wanted to do. So, I held my big picture clearly in my vision. I then ignored the dangerous middle ground. As I climbed that first hill, the Col de la Croix Fry, I realized that were I to try and concentrate on the second hill or the third hill at this point I was merely going to demotivate myself and doubt my ability to finish, and probably talk myself into quitting and therefore failing my challenge. But what I could do was create momentum by creating micro goals. Remind myself why I was doing this, to inspire other people, and then achieve my next micro goal. The more physically tired I became, or the more doubt that crept into my mind, the smaller I made each target and micro goal. So, in other words, I kept pulling the target closer and closer towards myself whilst all the time making sure that I was stepping forwards. It didn't matter how slowly I was going forwards, it just mattered that I was taking very small steps, or in this case pedal strokes, in a direction towards the end game. As I felt stronger or more motivated, I would open those goals, and increase my momentum, again, focusing on my why and my big picture. I have found this approach of avoiding the dangerous middle ground to be incredibly successful, and I've used it since L'Etape du Tour on several occasions in order to keep myself moving.

To put this into a business context, if you're set a seemingly huge target or project to achieve, remind yourself why. What is your in order to? What is your key role in achieving this objective? Then set yourself and your team micro goals along the way. Try not to get bogged down in the seemingly big tasks or hurdles that stand between you and the outcome, but rather keep taking small steps and maintain momentum with your team towards each of those micro goals along the way. If your team is achieving success and it's going well, move the goalposts further out and create greater momentum. If things are not going your way, it's important to maintain momentum, so bring those goals closer towards the team. A good analogy for this is push starting a car. To initially get the car started requires an awful lot of effort and for all that amount of effort the car seems to move incredibly slowly. As it starts to gain momentum, it becomes easier to push. You can see success in your sights, so you push harder, the car accelerates and, all being well, starts. This is a similar philosophy to maintaining momentum with our team when we come under pressure, or to use the expression I like, when the dark clouds start to roll in.

#BecauseICan – L'Etape Du Tour

L'Étape du Tour (French for "stage of the Tour") is an organized mass participation cycle event that allows amateur cyclists to race over the same route as a Tour de France stage. First held in 1993, and now organized by the Amaury Sport Organisation (ASO), in conjunction with *Vélo Magazine*, it takes place each July, normally on a Tour rest day. L'Étape du Tour is normally held over mountain roads in either the Pyrenees or French Alps, up climbs such as the Col du Galibier, Col d'Aubisque, Mont Ventoux or the Col du Tourmalet. Around 15,000 riders participate – many travelling from other countries to compete – and the event takes place on roads closed by the police to other traffic, with refreshment stops and medical support provided along the route.

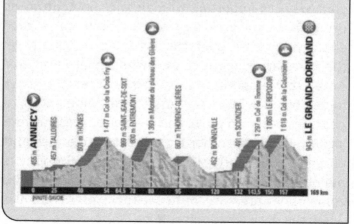

So what?

When faced with a situation where it feels like you can't succeed, remind yourself and your teammates why you undertook the challenge or task in the first place. Don't focus on the seemingly daunting elements of the challenge. Find yourself or your team a series of micro goals. They should be short term and achievable. This will help you to keep moving forwards and maintain momentum.

- Take small steps towards the big picture
- Focus on what you can achieve
- Extend and contract your goals to maintain momentum
- Keep moving forward no matter how slowly.

A bad day is normal

One of my co-directors, Paul Horwood (we served alongside each other in Afghanistan and climbed the Matterhorn together), likes to remind me that for every entrepreneur that is successful, for every Richard Branson or Elon Musk, there are probably 100 more that for various reasons, not always within their control, didn't get there. The same is true of expeditions and challenges. For every team member that I've accompanied up the side of a mountain on a long cycle or soon to be racing motorbikes in the desert there are probably four or five others that for various reasons were unable to see the task through. This is also certainly true of selection for specialist military units. I believe that one of the biggest reasons for this is what the military refer to as a VW (or voluntary withdrawal). In other words, you didn't fail, the instructor never told you that you weren't good enough, but in fact you decided that you were not up to the task and took yourself off the course. This often stems from having a bad day. For whatever reason, on a particular day or at a particular moment, your performance isn't as good as you think it would have been. You're feeling low. You tell yourself you can't do it, and much like my L'Etape du Tour experience, you begin to talk yourself out of the challenge. It is therefore important to understand that having a bad day doesn't mean you're a failure, the weakest link, or indeed have any sort of mental health problems. It simply means that you're having a bad day.

I have always really enjoyed watching the Olympic Games. I draw inspiration and motivation from watching people of all different shapes and sizes across a variety of sports achieve lifelong ambitions. In fact, during London 2012, I was serving in Afghanistan, and often late at night, battle-weary, soldiers would crowd around whatever television we could find to watch Olympic athletes push themselves as hard as they could and carry the national flag across the line. Watching Chris Hoy win his gold medal will live with me forever. Often, I find the backstories of how the athlete has overcome funding problems, training difficulties or disabilities even more inspiring than the final performance itself. One of the biggest revelations of the Tokyo 2020 (2021) Olympic Games has been the emergence of athletes being more comfortable to talk about the adversities that they face, not just physically but psychologically. Probably the most famous being Simone Biles. The American athlete is possibly one of the greatest gymnasts of all time, and certainly of her generation. She withdrew from a number of events in order to put her psychological well-being first. The point we're trying to make here is that even athletes at the very top of their game have a bad day.

In order to compensate for the feeling of inadequacy we experience when we start to have a bad day, or our performance dips, it is important to set expectations or to put everything into context. Earlier in this section, we talked about L'Etape du Tour and climbing Mount Everest. Although both extreme examples, the theory stands good. L'Etape took me approximately 10 hours of constant cycling, and on average it takes two months to climb Mount Everest. Sitting at home in my office, it makes complete sense to understand that there is no way I can cycle for 10 hours without experiencing some low points along the way and that it is even more unlikely that I can find myself on the side of Mount Everest in temperatures as low as minus 30 degrees centigrade and winds up to 100 miles an hour and not experience feelings of failure and self-doubt. We often hear athletes talking about being mentally tired. If we break this down, and gather intelligence information, it becomes obvious that regardless of aptitude or ability, training six hours a day, every day, demanding the ultimate performance day in, day out is going to take its toll. It's not realistic to expect that every single day feels like living the dream. The same is true in a business context: if we're working under pressure against stiff targets in an ever-changing environment, it stands to reason that not every day is going to be perfect. We are not always going to be on the top of our game. Social media can often be a double-edged sword. On the one hand it enables us to share our stories, tips, and advice with a wide-reaching audience. It also enables us to grab inspiration and motivation from those around us. There is, however, a tendency to only see what we want to see and to perceive the shiny, everything's perfect heroism of Olympic athletes. Expedition leaders and business influences have a tendency to assume that these individuals don't have bad days! They do!

#BecauseICan – Simone Biles

Simone Arianne Biles (born March 14, 1997) is an American artistic gymnast. With a combined total of 32 Olympic and World Championship medals, Biles is tied with Larisa Latynina as the most decorated gymnast of all time. Biles' seven Olympic medals also equal Shannon Miller for the most Olympic medals won by an American female gymnast. Biles is considered one of the greatest and most dominant gymnasts of all time. At the 2016 Summer Olympics in Rio de Janeiro, Biles won individual gold medals in the all-around, vault and floor; bronze on balance beam; and gold as part of the United States team, dubbed the "Final Five". At the 2020 Summer Olympics in Tokyo, she won bronze on balance beam, as well as silver with the United States team, after struggling with "the twisties", a temporary loss of air balance awareness. Her partial withdrawal, focus on safety, mental health and perseverance were praised. Biles is also a five-time world all-around champion, five-time world floor exercise champion, three-time world balance beam champion, two-time world vault champion, a seven-time United States national all-around champion and a member of the gold medal-winning American teams at the 2014, 2015, 2018 and 2019 World Artistic Gymnastics Championships.

One of the techniques that we can use to overcome these problems is to prepare ourselves or to set our level of expectation before we start. In other words, as a group or team, we sit down and in the same way that we discuss the physical problems and challenges that we're going to face, and likely to incur, we do the same thing with any psychological challenges that we are likely to incur. As a team of mountaineers, before setting foot on any mountain, we sit down and we say to each other at some point that we are all going to have lows and highs. We are all going to have days when we are strong and feeling good, and we're all going to have days when we accept that we're going to feel low, or feel like not going on and maybe even questioning why we were there in the first place. We then reassure each other that this is completely normal. It doesn't mean that we're failing, and it doesn't mean that we're having mental health issues. It simply means that we're having a bad day, and that is okay. In fact, were you to spend up to 60 days on the side of a mountain in minus 30 degrees temperature and not question yourself so much as once, one might argue that then there probably is something wrong with you.

This acceptance that it's completely normal to have a bad day can be a vital tool in our armour. At the point at which we are feeling low or like we want to give up, we remind ourselves that we knew this was going to happen and that it is an expected outcome of the circumstances that we are in. This helps to normalize and rationalize the feelings we are experiencing. We should then share our feelings with our teammates. It is extremely difficult to help someone if you aren't aware that they are suffering. The purpose of our Everest 15 expedition was to persuade as many service people as possible to ask for help when they need it.

Most of us have been for a hill walk or a run with a group of people. We have found ourselves struggling to keep up with the group, feeling as though we are struggling and the weakest link. Eventually, the person next to us turns and confesses that they are finding things hard and that they are not sure if they can continue. You instantly feel better about yourself and adopt a supportive role, probably sharing your own fears and concerns. This simple act of communication relieves the pressure on all parties. It's ok to ask for help! All of the most high-performance teams that I have been a member of have at least one thing in common. They are always confident in sharing with their teammates when they are experiencing a bad day. They are operating in a psychologically safe space.

When you're trying to combat long-term exposure to anxiety and pressure, see it for what it is and forgive yourself. It is completely okay to have a down day, to take your foot off the gas and to recoup. In the section about avoiding the dangerous middle ground, we discussed creating momentum and setting achievable targets. When I am experiencing a down day, one of the things I do is perform simple, often menial tasks. They are usually admin-related and the type of job that regularly gets bumped off the priority list. As they are simple to perform and not necessarily related to the tasks that are causing stress, they provide the opportunity to recover whilst providing the sense that I am moving towards my end goal.

Throughout 2020 and 2021 we have been delivering #BecauseICan workshops to schools, and we've spoken to over 3,000 school children. The children have been home-studying and missing a great deal of the interaction that they would normally expect when bouncing around the playground, sharing common rooms, or a classroom with their fellow students and teachers. It is therefore wholly unrealistic to think that they're psychological well-being is going to be anything other than changed from what it was before. This is not to say that it's better or worse, just different. If we've been sat alone, looking at a screen in our bedrooms doing our study, isolated, it is normal to expect us to have to have some bad days. We received a great deal of feedback from the students saying that their greatest anxiety was coming from having no frame of reference and no understanding of expectations. In other words, if they were finding their studies hard one day or missing their friends, they were convincing themselves that they were coping worse than everybody else and falling behind. This in turn led to them being embarrassed and not wanting to share their experiences with friends. They needed permission to have a bad day!

We've looked at several topics designed to help us deal with increasing pressure in varying environments. We've looked at avoiding the dangerous middle ground; understanding our why and enabling resilience wherever possible. Of course, this is not always going to be possible and, on occasion, we're going to have a bad day.

So what?

When setting out on any form of challenge and project, ensure that you and your team discuss what happens when you have a bad day. Do this before it happens. Remind yourself that it is unrealistic to think that you can undertake any long-term challenge and not have days when you question yourself and your motivations. This is normal. When experiencing a tough day, try to see it for what it is and accept the emotions that you are feeling. If at all possible, talk to a fellow team member.

- Set expectation levels
- Wanting to quit is normal
- Doubting yourself is usual, especially in high stress situations
- Find a way to move towards an outcome
- Focus on being part of the solution.

Part 5

FOCUS ON THE PEOPLE FIRST

In this final section of the book, we're going to look at possibly the most important factor enabling us to be effective – that is, influencing relationships and building a team of empowered people. In my experience, no matter how frightening or high pressure the challenges that we face, the solution has always been provided as a result of effective collaboration and strong relationships. No matter how large the corporations that are doing a deal, the contract is inevitably signed by a small group of people who have been able to communicate effectively, build a relationship, develop trust, and therefore sign a contract. In the often-murky world of intelligence operations, the capability of modern technology is simply staggering. What can be achieved with modern satellites, drones, and IT equipment, I will leave to your imagination. But no matter how high tech the equipment, the initial point of contact almost always starts with a relationship between two people. The handler builds trust with the agent who provides the phone numbers and locations for the technology.

Our ability to deal with high-pressure situations, to reach goals and to overcome problems is directly related to our ability to influence, support, and, when necessary, lead other people. In this section of the book, we're going to have a look at the difference between management and leadership. We're going to look at how best to lead people in high-pressure situations and we're going to understand a little more about rapport and influence.

Build rapport

The ability to build rapport in diverse situations with as many different people as possible is critical to our ability to create influence, and ultimately to be effective. Rapport is a term that we often hear used during sales training events, or when we talk about influence, but rarely do we sit down and think about what it actually means or how we go about achieving it. Ask yourself how I achieve rapport. If I was to walk into a completely cold situation with a new group of people, say a company conference, or a network meeting, how would I even start? Where would I begin to build rapport with the group of people in front of me?

First, it helps to understand what rapport is and where it comes from. There are several myths often quoted based around our ability to build rapport. The first is that we need to find something in common with the person we want to build rapport with. We're often told by glib sales trainers that we should seek out common ground with the person with which we're trying to build rapport, whether that's the football, cricket, our pet dog, or our family circumstances. This is, in fact, not true. Many of us will have been in a situation where we've been invited as a plus one to a wedding or a party. This is brilliant news. The alcohol is, invariably, free of charge. The music is retro, and there are relatively few people there that will know us; therefore the only person we are likely to embarrass is the person that invited us, and ourselves! Having danced yourself to exhaustion, you decide to make your way to the bar. Whilst standing at the bar, you turn to your right and see another stranger in a similar situation and strike up a conversation. It turns out that both of you support the same football team. Twenty minutes pass by and you have discussed your favourite players, what tactics should be being used, and who should be signed for the following season.

Eventually, you take your drinks, and you go back to your friend, the one who invited you to the party in the first place. As you have your drinks, your friend turns to you and says: "Who was that person you were talking to at the bar?" You reply, "I have no idea!" Your friend then points out that you were talking for nearly half an hour and asks what their name was? Again, you reply that you have absolutely no idea. Quite a lot of people reading this book right now will have found themselves in exactly this situation. In other words, you absolutely had something in common with the person that you were talking to but made little or no attempt to build rapport with that person, during the entire 20-minute conversation. It's worth noting, at this point, that having something in common with somebody can, and is, a very useful tool when looking to start up a conversation with somebody, but it does not necessarily help you progress towards building rapport. If having something in common with someone is not the answer to building rapport, what is it that we need to find, in order to achieve this level of influence? What we're looking for or listening for are shared beliefs and motivations. In other words, it is the "why" somebody supports a particular team or "why" they carry out a particular activity that will enable us to understand where the opportunity lies to build rapport with that person. As an example, sticking with the footballing theme, the person we're talking to tells us that they support Manchester United and go to every home game. You, like me, know little or nothing about football. The first important lesson is not to try and bluff.

The only thing I know about football is what I see on the news or the television reports. If I was talking to a football fan and trying to pretend that I knew about the game, it would not take them long to realize that I was trying to bluff. Some people will tell you that you should never have a negative when you're trying to build rapport with somebody. This is not true. It is much more important to be authentic. In this example, my response to being told that the person I am talking to is a fan is to explain that I'm terribly sorry and that I know nothing about football at all. Whilst I may seemingly have blown my initial ability to build rapport, what I have done is taken a step towards trust. I've been honest and told the person I'm talking to that I know little about their chosen subject. They are now more likely to believe me when I tell them that I do know about a different topic.

What I want to find out is why they support Manchester United. Remember, what we're looking for are shared beliefs and motivations.

The person I'm talking to explains to me that they work very long hours and often take the children to sports clubs on a Sunday but that they attend every home game. The home game is their time to themselves and provides a chance to escape and to recharge. The key factor here in building rapport is the belief that they need to have some time to themselves. The reason this individual explained to me that they worked hard and helped look after the family is that they were looking for permission to have time to themselves. In response, the first thing I would say is "Of course, everybody needs some time to themselves". I've just authenticated this individual and given them permission to share their belief with me. This is our first step towards building rapport. I explain to them that whilst I'm not into football, I am into motorcycles and when I go for a ride, I also enjoy time to myself and a chance to recharge. We're now building rapport around the shared motivation and belief that we need to find time for ourselves. In other words, we're building rapport around the shared beliefs and motivations of time to ourselves, and it is irrelevant that we are talking about football and riding motorcycles. In order to discover these beliefs and motivations, it is really important that we listen as closely and intently as we can. I'm sure all of us at some stage have been on an active listening course.

You will have been taught to make all sorts of "listening" noises, accompanied by appropriate head shakes and nods. In fact, this is not enough. We need to encourage or spin a conversation in order to get the other person talking as much as possible. If we ask a direct question, we will get a direct answer and we are much less likely to be able to identify somebody's beliefs or motivations. Ask yourself whether you've been involved in a conversation that went something like this.

> **You**: "I understand that you've just come back from your holiday?"

> **Them**: "Yes. I've just been to Switzerland for the first time."

> **You**: "Oh, fantastic. Switzerland is one of my favourite places in the world. I love Geneva."

Our intent is to build rapport and we believe that by explaining that we've also been to Switzerland, and it's one of our favourite places that we are sharing that experience, and therefore building rapport. In fact, what we've done is hijack the conversation, and made it about our experiences of Switzerland, rather than theirs. What we're trying to do is to get the other person to continue talking as much as is possible and therefore place them in a situation where they are more likely to reveal personal beliefs and motivations. We can achieve this by spinning the conversation. We repeat back keywords or phrases or mirror sections of the conversation. In this example, I would repeat back to the person the word 'Switzerland'. They inevitably then expand upon Switzerland, and why they had visited, sharing with us beliefs, and motivations as to why that destination appealed to them. All the time we are listening and looking for an opportunity to match those beliefs and motivations.

If we're not comfortable repeating back specific words then we can use what we call "encourages". In other words, we can say things like;

go on
and so
go on
tell me more

You will notice that what we're not doing is asking any more questions. Many of us will have been taught that there are two types of question: closed questions, which require a yes or no answer, or open questions that often begin with one of the following words:

what

where

when

why

Whilst these open questions will certainly provoke a more long-winded answer, and enable the person who we're talking to to further discuss their beliefs or opinions, they can seem like an interrogation and can often provide the person you're talking to the opportunity to shut us down. Again, this is not what we're trying to achieve if we're trying to understand the person's beliefs or motivations.

Using our example of Switzerland, what this person said was that they had been to Switzerland for the first time. I can now use a combination of these techniques. I can reply:

"Switzerland (*pause*) for the first time (*pause*). Tell me more."

This person will then explain to me where they had been before and what were their motivations for changing to Switzerland, thus enabling me more opportunity to build rapport and get a wider understanding of their beliefs and motivations. It is entirely possible for us to build rapport with people that we don't particularly like. Just because we wouldn't want to share a meal or go for a drink with somebody doesn't mean that we don't have shared beliefs around family values, or a strong sense of purpose. One of the most extreme courses that I have ever been on is called resistance to interrogation.

This course does exactly what it says on the tin! It would be inappropriate for me to go into the specific details here. Needless to say, we found ourselves in a highly pressured confrontational situation. Whilst we were aware that this was a training exercise and not real, we were aware that as special duties operators, we were volunteering to put ourselves into situations where this level of training may become necessary. Even during the most extreme of circumstances, we were taught, wherever possible, to try and build rapport with our captors. Even when faced with an aggressor, who was seeking to break us and extract intelligence, we were taught to remain as calm as possible, to seek out shared beliefs and motivations with our interrogators and to use these techniques to build rapport as effectively and as best we could. Once you've established rapport with somebody, it makes it ever more difficult to force confrontation with them. Whenever I find myself in any form of negotiation, business development meeting, or large conference environment, my primary objective is to build rapport with the people that I need to interact with all day long. Even before we talk about business contracts or opportunities, my priority is always to understand somebody's beliefs and motivations, and to listen as intently as I can to those around me. Time spent listening and building rapport with the people around you will never be wasted.

- Listen to and encourage the conversation
- You are listening for beliefs and motivations
- You don't need something in common
- Try not to talk for more than 20% of the time.

Management v leadership

Whenever I talk about management or leadership, I am talking about the verb, or the action of managing or leading. The current corporate world in which we operate can be somewhat confusing. Business cards say partner when they mean director or director when they mean manager. We often talk about management and leadership in the same sentence as though it's merely a difference of terminology. One of the lessons that I've learned in order to be more effective is you need to separate the two disciplines of management and leadership. They are both equally important, and as an expedition leader team member, or professional individual, you are certainly going to need to do both. It's also worth understanding that you don't have to have a manager or leader in your title in order to be expected to lead, or manage. Often a situation or a project needs leading, and people will always look to be led.

So, what is the difference between the two? I believe that management is anything to do with systems, processes or key performance indicators. It is the stuff of business or the stuff of project management. It provides the feedback loops, the processes and the measurement by which we can judge whether a particular project or task we are engaged in is on target to achieve the required outcome. Leadership is anything to do with people. Anything to do with vision, motivation and inspiration falls under the leadership bracket. I'm going to suggest that from now on, having read this book, you're going to wear one of two caps; you are always going to be having to wear one of the two caps, but you can't wear them both together, largely because you look stupid. So in other words, you're always going to be wearing either the management hat or the leadership hat. If the problem that you're trying to solve requires a change in process or system or needs you to put in place some form of measurement, you're going to have your management hat on. Your outcome is inevitably going to be one of creating a system or a process. You'll collaborate with as many people as possible, usually subject matter experts, and you will create a measurement and a feedback loop. If you're seeking to motivate, to inspire a group of people or to support a group of people during difficult circumstances, then you're definitely going to have to put on your leadership cap. In any given circumstance, the first thing to ask yourself is whether the problem I'm facing is one of management, or is it one of leadership? In most high-pressure situations or challenging environments, I have found that you need to wear your leadership cap first. If you can get the people on side, the systems, processes, and numbers will almost certainly take care of themselves.

Recently, we've created a culture of trying to lead with KPIs and figures. The targets and numbers merely show the leader whether what they are doing is being effective or not. Take an athlete: in telling that athlete that in order to win the race they need to run faster, this achieves very little. They are still none the wiser as to what they need to do or how they need to achieve it. By telling them to run faster, you're merely increasing the pressure on the individual. You're trying to lead them with a management figure or number. This will never be effective. If you're able to inspire and motivate the people, then it is entirely possible that the numbers will take care of themselves.

We've all been to the annual company conference where various senior members of the team have taken it in turn to stand on stage and deliver their keynote speech or message. Often we leave these conferences slightly confused, somewhat overloaded and not entirely sure as to the required outcome we are supposed to achieve at the conference. This is often because the messaging has been a mix of management and leadership, and therefore the outcome has not been clear. How many times have you listened to a sales director attempting to motivate or inspire a team by using a graph or chart? How often have you seen a systems analyst show a flow diagram and then describe it as inspirational? We can be far more effective if we divide these two functions, and deliver specific messaging under either the management, or the leadership headings. Do the two things separately. This may mean that you have to hold two separate meetings or deliver two separate messages, but that is okay, and will still be clearer and more effective than confusing the two. Ask yourself, what is the outcome that you're trying to achieve? If the outcome is based around motivation, inspiration or you're trying to unite a team, then make sure you start by putting on your leadership cap and deliver vision and inspiration.

You will need to do both management and leadership in order to be successful, but we can go about the two things entirely differently. Imagine, if you will, Martin Luther King comes into work one day and proclaims to the office that he has a dream. Everybody is initially excited, highly motivated, and looking forward to hearing about this dream. The following day, Martin Luther comes in and announces that he has another dream. The workforce is still motivated and interested and thinks Martin must be having a great week. By Wednesday and then subsequently Thursday we are on dream number four and the team has now lost interest. There's no detail. There are no specifics and, in fact, when Martin announces the fact that he has another dream the team quietly asks him to go about his business and leave them to do theirs. By the same token, had he come in first thing on Monday morning, and announced that he had a plan, then many of the team would have been disinterested, asked him to make the tea and gone about their own business. This was not exciting enough to grab their attention. So, in other words, what he needed to do was put on his leadership cap on Monday morning, and announce to the team that he had a dream. When he came in on Tuesday morning, he needed to change that cap to a management cap and explain to the team that he had a plan in order to carry out that dream. Once the plan had been in place for a few days, and the team were perhaps losing the vision of what it was that needed to be achieved, or why they were doing it, he may then take off his management hat, put his leadership hat back on, and reignite the flame of the dream. Thus, you can see how moving between management and leadership in clear, distinct phases enables you to keep the team operating as effectively as it possibly can.

- Wear either your leadership hat or your management hat not both together
- Lead first
- You manage systems and processes; you lead people
- KPIs tell you whether the leadership is effective.

Provide reassurance and direction

Many of us have found ourselves in a situation where we've been newly promoted, recently started a new project, or have begun planning for our next adventure, and we hit that glass ceiling: the moment in which the initial excitement has worn off. We find our first stumbling blocks, and suddenly this whole thing doesn't seem like quite such a good idea. In this section of the book, we're going to have a look at a couple of top tips as to how to maintain momentum, manage the project, and lead the people, in order to keep heading towards that final goal.

There is a commonly held myth that in high-pressure situations, the only form of leadership that works is what we would often refer to as pacesetting: a first in, last out, be better at everything than everybody else and be by far and away the leading example for each of the team members-type attitude. This has its place, and there are certain occasions when this might work. My experience is that it is demotivating and, in fact, widens the gap between the leader and those being led. Often, when team members who are having a bad day see somebody who appears to be invulnerable charging ahead and impervious to all the pressures and stresses that are happening around them, rather than motivating and inspiring them to do better, it underlines and confirms the fact that they are struggling, and the weakest member of the team. If our outcome is to relieve pressure to get our team operating and thinking back to the best of its ability, then in fact, this kind of pacesetting style can have the exact opposite effect to the one that we need to achieve. We also must consider whether we need to manage or lead any given situation, and we've looked at the pros and cons of each, in the previous section.

During this section of the book, we're primarily dealing with when the pressure comes on, the momentum has stalled, or we find ourselves in an unexpected, perhaps even crisis, situation. We are going to need to manage, for sure, but initially, leadership becomes more important. It's vital that we motivate, inspire, and lead the people initially, and then put in place the required management KPIs and processes in order to ensure that we continue to maintain momentum. The first important factor here is that the leader doesn't necessarily have to have all the answers. In any one of the situations I have found myself in, very rarely have I had the answer: almost by definition, a high-pressure crisis situation doesn't have a specific or clear answer. The leader's job is to get the team operating together, enable the team to be part of the solution. It is, in fact, way more valuable for the leader to be approachable, and often a little vulnerable. Whilst the team is under pressure, the fight or flight mechanism that we discussed earlier in this book will be in full effect, and members of the team will be experiencing anxiety, and occasionally analysis paralysis.

Using our analogy from earlier in the book, we need to put up the umbrella and relieve the pressure on the team. It's vital at this stage that the team feel comfortable in approaching us and talking to us. In my view, there is nothing wrong with saying to the team that you are finding this situation scary or you in fact can't necessarily see the clear answer. In other words, be just a little vulnerable, align yourself with the team and close the gap between the leader and the led. Being vulnerable doesn't mean that you must burst into tears. It just simply means you demonstrate to the team that you are human; and you are managing to deal with the situation; therefore they also will be able to deal with this situation. When the catastrophic thinking cycle begins, the false expectation drives our thought processes, and we find ourselves thinking this might happen, this could happen, and if this happens that will lead to that happening. So initially, in these high-pressure situations, the leader needs to reassure their team. Reassuring the team is different to providing the specific answer or solution. Explain to them that we're going to look after each other, remind them that they are the best possible group of people to be in this situation. We've worked together for however long and we are going to fix this together. Reassure individuals that nobody's going to become isolated or left behind. Reassurance is simply that, as the leader, I am on your side, we're working together, and nobody is being left behind. In other words, we're dealing with the team's primal fears and appealing to the five core concerns we all face in high-pressure, or crisis situations.

Appreciation	Am I valued?
Affiliation	Am I part of the team?
Autonomy	Do I have control?
Status	Am I failing / succeeding?

Role   Do I have a direction or purpose?

The next key factor for us is to provide direction. One of the frightening statistics surrounding high-altitude mountaineering and the number of adventurers that become lost in remote locations is that they appear to simply run out of energy and perhaps, more importantly, run out of ideas. They are found where it appears as though they have simply sat down and accepted their fate. It is vital as a leader in a high-pressure situation that we don't allow individual team members to accept their own fate and to sit down and become a passenger. What we need to do is provide direction for the task ahead. It may seem as though providing direction is the last thing either the leader or those being led want to do. But, in fact, it will provide us with a purpose, and enable us to be part of the solution.

I'm sure during the early days of the pandemic, we will all remember the seemingly crazy shopping sprees that were going on. People buying hundreds of toilet rolls or pints and pints of milk. I'm sure that none of those individuals believed they were actually going to need all of that toilet roll or drink all of that milk. What they're doing is expressing a basic human need to get control of the situation. We as human beings don't like the sensation that we're out of control. We will continue to come down a ladder of priorities and needs until we can find something that gives us that sense of control back again. In other words, when members of the public were told you will be locked down, you won't be working, you'll be going home, you may only go shopping for necessities, there was a sense of losing control. All these factors are outside of the individual's control. Suddenly, bulk buying items makes the individual feel as though they are back in control, and they've got a purpose.

As a leader or a senior team member, we can help with this situation by providing specific direction. As an example, I mentioned earlier in the book that our Everest expedition in 2015 didn't end well. After the earthquakes and a secondary quake had struck, the area turned into a massive disaster zone. Our climbing expedition had now turned into a humanitarian rescue mission, and an exercise in us escaping through China. All our routes home had been removed. Entire towns had slipped into river gorges and all the roads and checkpoints that we had used to get from Kathmandu through Tibet to Everest base camp were now gone. It would have been very easy for us to simply sit down and accept our fate. What we did was focus on what we could do. We reunited our team, who were split up at the time. We focused on what we did have available, that is, tents, equipment and rations. We concentrated on what solutions were available to us: what were the routes home, what communications did we have and who were we able to talk to or collaborate with in order to gain wider assistance. Each team member was given a specific task and responsibility for a given area of the project. At no stage did the team sit down and accept what was happening to it. But instead, we did our best to become a part of the solution.

By becoming part of the solution, we feel as though we're gaining control of that situation, the fight or flight reaction slowly starts to dissipate and we're able to think wider than we were before. As part of our escape and evasion training, we were taught that in a captivity situation there are only three possible courses of action. Imagine that you've been locked into a room. The first possible course of action is that you simply go into denial, and you pretend that this is not happening to me and it's not real. I'm going to wake up in a minute and somebody's just going to open that door, and it will all be fine. This is possibly the most dangerous course of action and the one most likely to cause traumatic side effects to the individual.

The second course of action is what I would refer to as enduring. You accept the fact that you've been locked into this room, and that that situation is outside of your control. You set up psychological games and tools that will enable you to endure this situation. There are various accounts of long-term prisoners of war who talk about things like building their perfect house, one brick at a time, in their minds, or go on that perfect road trip. I would argue that during the pandemic we have seen a number of these coping strategies put into place, whether that's quizzes, group choirs, or social Zoom meetings. In my view, the endure mindset is a distinct improvement over the "this is not happening to me" mindset but is still not ideal. We're not taking control of our own fate and we're certainly not becoming part of the solution; we are relying on somebody coming and opening the door for us. We are giving up control and direction of our own fate.

The third and most challenging mindset to adopt is one where, from the moment the door is closed behind us, we are planning to escape. We don't know how or when we will be able to do that, but we're going to gather intelligence, and constantly be part of the solution. We're going to look for opportunity and build up a picture of the environment around us. Whilst on occasion this may seem hopeless, the reality of this psychological strategy is that we are always being part of the solution and we are fighting towards that outcome.

The same is true in any number of high-pressure situations. We can reassure the team that it is going to be okay and we're going to find a way out of this and we're going to work together to achieve that. We then provide direction towards that solution. We intelligence gather, remembering that it must be accurate, timely and relevant. We focus entirely on what we can do and what is available to us, and we feed that back into our OODA loop this decision-making cycle. That direction, in turn, keeps us moving slowly, one step at a time, towards the outcome. As a leader, or senior team member, if we're able to do this, the motivation and morale of the team will remain considerably higher than if we adopt any of the previous strategies.

So what?

The movies would have us believe that when leading a team or involved in a high-pressure situation we need to be an invulnerable, indestructible leader. This is not true. Being approachable will narrow the gap between those who are struggling and those who are feeling strong. This unifies the team, relieves pressure and increases the chances of success. Where possible, focus on providing the team with a constructive purpose and help them to be part of the solution.

- You don't need to be a Spartan leader
- Provide reassurance and direction
- Don't be afraid to be vulnerable
- Close the gap between the leader and the led.

CONCLUSION: THINK IN CIRCLES AND SELECT THE RIGHT TOOL FOR THE JOB

Remember that everything we've discussed in this book starts with using intelligence, not information. We must filter all the background information and turn it into intelligence. It must be accurate, timely and relevant. Anything else we do from that point – collaboration, negotiation, presentation, and occasionally deal with confrontation – will work better if we are only using and communicating the intelligence. Do your absolute best to not do whatever it is that you've done before for the sake of it. React to what's happening around you, and what is real, rather than your perception of it. Don't just put in place strategies that worked the last time we did this, or at my last place of work. Use the OODA loop thinking model and effective collaboration as tools to empower colleagues and teammates. Rather than looking to give them an answer or micromanage them, we're looking to get them engaged and to become part of the solution within their own right. This in turn drives motivation and effective outcomes.

We need to accept the fact that in high-pressure situations, whether that's physical situations or high-pressure situations in a corporate environment, physiological changes take place in the body. Those physiological changes, the fight or flight mechanism, will happen to both us as leaders and team members, and will happen to our colleagues. This is not a personal choice, or somebody choosing to be difficult, but is in fact a reaction to a chemical change taking place inside the body.

The first thing you need to do in order to look after your teammates is to deal with that reaction. Allow them a moment. Take a tactical pause and understand what's happening to both them and you. Use your toolkit to help rationalize what is actually happening. The intelligence information mantra will greatly assist here. Remember if FEAR (False, Expectation, Appearing, Real) wins when the fight or flight mechanism has been triggered, we will go down a spiral of catastrophic thinking. We focus on what might happen, could happen or should happen, and all of the "what ifs". If we need our team to be released from the effects of the fight or flight mechanism and freed of analysis paralysis, we need to reduce pressure, not increase it. As a leader, or experienced team member, we're looking to put up that umbrella and create a safe space for our team to operate in. This in turn gives them the opportunity to start to think outside of the box and become part of the solution. In order to be truly effective, we need to become resilient. This is not a course or a qualification, but a long journey, and we can speed up that journey by ensuring each member of our team understands their why or their "in order to".

It is important that we focus on not simply the task, but why are we doing this task. What part or role does that task play in the much bigger picture? If we have a team of young people that need to feel empowered and as though they're contributing, delivering an effective "in order to" will achieve this. Try to avoid the dangerous middle ground. We do this by focusing on taking small steps towards the bigger picture, accepting the fact that along this journey it is completely normal to have a bad day. Set expectation levels. Explain to your team members that any complex, challenging, high-pressure task will inevitably lead to days when we question our motivation and question our ability to perform a task. This is completely normal. I mentioned David Brailsford who explained that motivation will ebb and flow daily, but provided commitment remains strong, we will achieve our outcome.

No matter what systems, processes or technology we utilize, always remember that people and relationships are the key to achieving the aim. Look to understand and support people's beliefs and motivations. In any situation, negotiation or even confrontation, understanding what it is that somebody else wants to achieve, how they are motivated or what they believe in will ultimately help us achieve our own outcomes and aims. Look upon these relationships like a bank account. If you want to make a withdrawal at some point prior to doing that, you have to have paid in. If you're going to go overdrawn, you're going to have to ensure that you pay that money back at some stage. Looking after your team and people is the same concept. It is important to pay into our team first. The Royal Military Academy Sandhurst's motto is, "serve to lead". In other words, the leader serves the team, and not the other way around. If we're going to make a particularly high expectation of our team and expect them to perform in either a dangerous, high-pressure situation, or simply need to stay extra-long hours, then we're going overdrawn. It's important that the top priority immediately following the situation is to pay back into that account. There is no need to be a Spartan leader. You're not expected to have all the answers in most high-pressure situations, it would be odd if you did. Lead first, then manage. If you inspire and motivate the people, the systems, processes and numbers stand a chance of taking care of themselves. Wherever you possibly can, provide reassurance and direction. Above all, try not to blindly follow a process. Remember that you are collecting a toolkit, and that utilizing OODA loop thinking will help you select the right tool at the right time to do the right job, empower both yourself and your team to be a part of the solution, regularly ask yourself, and encourage your team members to ask themselves that question: Am I being part of the solution? Am I working towards the aim?

Communicate – Communicate – Communicate
Be part of the solution
#BecauseICan

ABOUT THE AUTHOR

Timothy Bradshaw has never won the Olympics or sold a multimillion-pound business. He went to a reasonable school and attended the Royal Military Academy Sandhurst. Since then, he has served as a covert human intelligence officer, attempted to climb Mount Everest, summited the Matterhorn, completed a 70.3 ironman, cycled L'Etape du Tour, ridden the Cresta Run and set up an international business training consultancy, all #BecauseICan.

As a director of Sandstone Communications, Tim delivers keynote speaking and leadership training in over 14 different countries and to a global audience in excess of 5000 people annually. He has been listed as a leadership influencer by LinkedIn and LETG (the Legal, Education and Training Group).

He also sponsors aspiring young people striving to achieve their dreams and has spoken to thousands of schoolchildren, helping them to develop a #BecauseICan mindset.

Thanks to ...

The directors of Sandstone Communications – Cedric Astor, Paul Horwood and David Samuel – for allowing me to be me and always covering my blindspots.

Ed Mason, The Ice Room, for the illustrations and models. He has been key in creating our brand.

The Royal Military Academy Sandhurst – a great deal of what I've learned has been taught there.